Knut Hamsun
Remembers America

Knut Hamsun
Remembers America

Essays and Stories
1885–1949

TRANSLATED AND EDITED BY

Richard Nelson Current

UNIVERSITY OF MISSOURI PRESS
COLUMBIA AND LONDON

Copyright © 2003 by
The Curators of the University of Missouri
University of Missouri Press, Columbia, Missouri 65201
Printed and bound in the United States of America
All rights reserved
5 4 3 2 1   07 06 05 04 03

Library of Congress Cataloging-in-Publication Data

Hamsun, Knut, 1859–1952.
   Knut Hamsun remembers America : essays and stories, 1885–1949 /
translated and edited by Richard Nelson Current.
       v. cm.
Includes bibliographical references.
Contents: Critical reporting (1885–1888) — The American character —
New York City — Yellow Thunder's camp — Mark Twain — A bonanza
farm — Robert Ingersoll — Memory and fantasy (1897–1905) — Terror
— On the prairie — Zachæus — Vagabond days — A woman's victory
— Mellow reminiscence (1928, 1949) — Festina lente — My first time
abroad.
       ISBN 0-8262-1456-8 (alk. paper)
     1. Hamsun, Knut, 1859–1952—Journeys—United States.   2. United
States—Civilization.   I. Title.
PT8950.H3 K59 2003
839.8'28603—dc21

                                                            2002155800

    ⊗™ This paper meets the requirements of the
American National Standard for Permanence of Paper
for Printed Library Materials, z39.48, 1984.

Designer: Kristie Lee
Typesetter: The Composing Room of Michigan, Inc.
Printer and binder: The Maple-Vail Book Manufacturing Group
Typeface: Adobe Caslon

Frontispiece: Knut Hamsun in the uniform of a streetcar conductor,
Chicago, 1886. From Einar Skavlan, *Knut Hamsun*
(Oslo: Gyldendal, 1929), 113.

To the memory of my mother
née *Anna Christiansen (1889–1986)*
a daughter of Norway

CONTENTS

ACKNOWLEDGMENTS

Two people in particular made this book possible. Robert H. Ferrell, a friend for more than a half century, took an interest, sight unseen, in my manuscript and recommended it to his favorite publisher. Beverly Jarrett, director and editor in chief of the University of Missouri Press, responded with enthusiasm. She and members of her staff, especially copyeditor Gary Kass, proceeded efficiently to get the manuscript ready for publication.

Meanwhile, my physical therapist, Nancy Bonomi Eldridge, kept me in condition to continue working on the project. My wife and erstwhile co-author, Marcia A. Ewing-Current, gave me mobility and did the many chores incidental to writing and publishing that I could no longer do for myself.

To all these people, many thanks!

Knut Hamsun
Remembers America

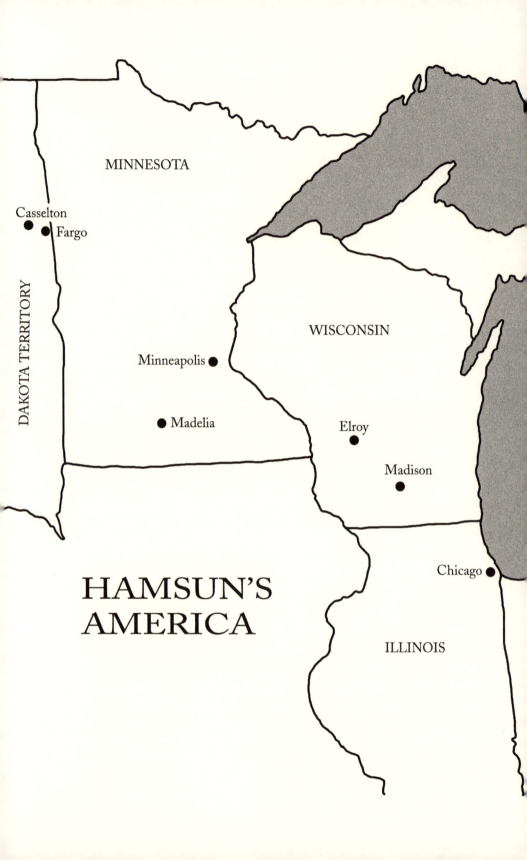

INTRODUCTION

Hamsun's America

When Americans remember him at all, they no doubt think of Knut Hamsun (1859–1952) as the author of *Hunger* or as the Norwegian who, along with Vidkun Quisling, betrayed his country by supporting the Nazis during World War II. Yet Hamsun, winner of the Nobel Prize in 1920 for his novel *Growth of the Soil,* was and remains one of the most important and influential novelists of his time, one who served as a model for many younger contemporaries, among them Ernest Hemingway. The young Hamsun in turn had looked to Mark Twain as a model. On the whole, however, he accumulated more negative than positive feelings for Americans and for American ways, while never losing the marks left by the early years he spent in the United States.

The First Visit, 1882–1884

Like others among the 29,000 Norwegians who migrated to America in 1882, the twenty-three-year-old Hamsun went with high hopes, which in his case were soon to turn into bitter disappointment.

Brought up in the arctic north of Norway, the son of an impecunious farmer and tailor, he had experienced a great deal of hard work but very little schooling. Still, he aspired with single-minded determination to become a writer, and he prepared for such a career by reading widely and by teaching himself proper Dano-Norwegian (essentially Danish), the literary language of the time and place. To further his studies, he received a gift

of money from a well-to-do businessman, and he wrote two rather sopho-
moric love stories that were published locally, in Tromsø (1877) and Bodø
(1878).

As author of the first of these books he was identified as Kn. Pedersen
and of the second as Knud Pedersen Hamsund, his patronymic being supplemented by a place name, that of the family farm. He was still common-
ly known, however, as Knud, or Knut, Pedersen. Not until 1885 was he to
fix his name and identity as Knut Hamsun (without the terminal *d*), though
he had used this form as early as 1880.

When his publications failed to advance his career, Hamsun was reduced
to rough physical labor as a member of a road construction crew. Inevitably
he thought of trying to better his luck in America, as so many of his fellow
Norwegians were trying to do. His older brother, Peter Pedersen, was already a resident of Elroy, Wisconsin. Bjørnstjerne Bjørnson, one of Norway's most famous authors, had recently returned from an American lecture tour to praise the United States as a land of opportunity. Hamsun went
to one of Bjørnson's speeches, made his acquaintance, and received his encouragement. Later Bjørnson wrote a letter of recommendation to America for Hamsun. Other friends helped to finance his travel, and the North
German Lloyd steamship line gave him not only free passage from Ham-
burg to New York but also money for a railroad ticket to Elroy—in return
for his promise to write an account of the voyage (which, if written, was
never published).

Landing in New York in January, the wide-eyed immigrant was overwhelmed by his first impressions of America. Here, as he wrote home, were
such wonders as an elevated railway, one that went "up in the air, above the
people's houses"; the Brooklyn Bridge, "the greatest engineering feat in the
world"; and buildings "thirteen stories high," with elevators. In the post office he was "shot up to the fourth floor in a kind of swaying contraption."

In Chicago he was similarly impressed. Of the new city hall, which occupied almost an entire block, he wrote: "It is the handsomest building I
have ever seen. The granite is so highly polished that we could see our re-
flections in it, and the ornamentation is pure art work from Europe." While
in Chicago, he submitted a couple of poems to the Norwegian-language
periodical *Norden*, which accepted them. His American adventure seemed
to be getting off to a good start.

After he reached Madison, Wisconsin, however, he ran into something of a setback. Here lived Rasmus B. Anderson, whom Bjørnson had met on his American tour and to whom he had addressed the letter recommending Hamsun. Anderson (1846–1936), the Wisconsin-born son of Norwegian immigrants, was professor of Scandinavian studies at the state university, author of books on Norwegian subjects, and a future American minister to Denmark. Rather self-important, he looked down on the ambitious young newcomer, thinking him brash for proposing to emulate the great Bjørnson with a lecture tour. Anderson offered little or no help or encouragement.

Hamsun was due for further disillusionment when, in February, he got off the train at Elroy. A town of about eight hundred people, Elroy owed such importance as it possessed to its location on a recently constructed line of the Chicago and North Western Railway. Here Hamsun quickly discovered that his brother could offer no assistance. Peter, seven years older and married to an American, was operating his own tailor shop but failing to make a go of it, fond as he was of both music and drink. A few months after Knut's arrival, Peter left Elroy to try his luck again in an even smaller Wisconsin town.

Meanwhile, Hamsun labored for subsistence at a succession of jobs in and around Elroy, first at a Norwegian-owned store in town and then on three nearby small farms, one after another, whose owners were scarcely better off than he was. By summer's end he was serving as a delivery boy at Harry Hart's general store, the biggest business in Elroy, and before long he was promoted to the comparatively remunerative and prestigious position of clerk.

He could now afford to live in a hotel if someone shared the room and expense with him, and he found Will T. Ager willing to do so. Ager, an American of British stock, about the same age as Hamsun, taught in the local high school. For several months the two roomed on the top floor of the C. & N. W. Railway Hotel, a large, three-story wooden building near the tracks on the side opposite the station.

Ager held his roommate in respect bordering on awe despite the man's eccentricities—or because of them. Hamsun struck him as tall, strong, well-built, handsome. With his long, "leonine" hair, chiseled features, and pince-nez glasses attached to a gold chain, he looked the part of the author he aspired to be. He possessed not only literary but also artistic talent, which he exercised on the low ceiling of the hotel room. Ager especially admired a "pencil drawing representing the Angel of Night spreading the veil of darkness over the world." This drawing so impressed the hotel manager that he often showed it to guests.

Hamsun had picked up some English on his various jobs, and Ager helped him to improve his command of the language, as did Henry M. Johnston, principal of the Elroy high school. He showed some progress when, in his excellent penmanship, he wrote on the plaster wall of the hotel room, beneath a sketch of his own profile: "My life is a peaceless flight through all the land. My religion is the Moral of the wildest Naturalism, but my world is the Aesthetical literature." When he asked Ager to edit the draft of a story in English, however, Ager gave up, judging the composition so unidiomatic as to be hopeless.

Meanwhile Hamsun was busily writing in his own language and, after nine months in the United States, was finally ready to start his lecturing career. In a country schoolhouse near Elroy he spoke on Bjørnson to a packed house of Norwegian Americans. Reporting the occasion in its issue of November 8, 1882, the Wisconsin Norwegian-language newspaper *Skandinaven* praised him as a well-informed and effective speaker: "It is to be hoped that the Scandinavians around Elroy will take advantage of the opportunity to hear Mr. Hamsund (if he appears again), especially since 'Admission is free.'" Thus his first lecture, unremunerative as it was, could be considered no more than a qualified success.

Still, he was encouraged to try again. Soon after Christmas he wrote to Professor Anderson to ask his advice and help in getting a speaking engagement in Madison or Stoughton, each of which towns contained a much larger Norwegian population than could be found in the Elroy area. Whether with Anderson's help or not, Hamsun was invited to Stoughton, where in April 1883 he spoke in Opera Hall on Bjørnson and Norwegian politics. Only about twenty persons came to hear him. *Skandinaven* attributed the small turnout to bad weather, but Hamsun blamed Stoughton and its people. "All they know about is drinking," he complained to Anderson. "The place is a shithole."

Later that spring he nevertheless made one more appearance as a lecturer in Wisconsin. At the end of the school year he accompanied Ager on a visit to the latter's home and parents in Briggsville, on Lake Mason. Appearing at the nearby Beaver Valley School, Hamsun gave a third lecture on Bjørnson. Ager attended, and though he could not understand a word he listened raptly for two hours, fascinated by his friend's speaking voice, gestures, and stage presence. While in Briggsville, the two men visited a nearby Indian camp, which fascinated Hamsun.

After this vacation Hamsun went back to work for Harry Hart, who no longer owned the general store but still managed it. Hamsun was lifting a salt barrel into a wagon one day when something seemed to "tear loose" in his chest, and he hemorrhaged. This convinced him he must find a job that required less physical exertion. He saw no future for himself in Elroy, anyhow. Ager was thinking of moving west and Henry Johnston had already done so, leaving his position as school principal and buying a lumber business in Madelia, Minnesota. When Johnston offered him employment, Hamsun was ready to accept. He left Elroy near the end of 1883 after almost two years there.

In Madelia he met a man who was to do much more for him than anyone else in the United States had done. That man was Kristofer Janson, a preacher and writer from Norway, quite well known in Norwegian-American circles. A Unitarian, Janson was something of a circuit rider, serving a large congregation in Minneapolis, his headquarters, and smaller groups in other places, among them Madelia. Here he preached to as many as a hundred Norwegians at a time who forgathered from farms in the vicinity. He also debated spokesmen for the Norwegian Lutheran church, who denounced him as a heretic.

Hamsun took an interest in the debates, though he had no religious convictions whatsoever. Janson nevertheless offered him a job as his secretary in Minneapolis and easily convinced him that he should support himself by means of mental rather than physical work. The terms were attractive: Hamsun would live with the Janson family and would be paid $500 a year plus traveling expenses. So, after about three months in Madelia, he moved to Minneapolis.

A comparatively large and growing city and very much a Scandinavian center, Minneapolis offered a considerably wider scope for Hamsun than Elroy or Madelia had done. Soon he was deeply involved in the day-to-day activities of the Janson mission. He wrote (in Norwegian) a newspaper article defending Janson against attacks on his Unitarianism, gave lectures under his sponsorship, and substituted for him in the pulpit, though only to speak on secular topics. He also translated articles from English to Norwegian, but when he was assigned to translating them from Norwegian to English, the result was not good enough for Janson. Meanwhile, with the encouragement of Janson's wife, Drude, who found him charming, he read widely in Janson's library, including American literature.

While auctioneering at a church bazaar, Hamsun began to cough blood again. A Norwegian-American doctor, educated at the University of Copenhagen, gave a diagnosis of "galloping consumption" and a prognosis of death within a few months. Under Drude Janson's care Hamsun got better but not well, and by summer's end he decided to go home to die. The Jansons collected money for his fare. By the time he reached New York he had almost recovered from his illness, which proved to be nothing worse than a bad case of bronchitis. From New York he probably took the usual route to Norway: by ship to Liverpool, train to Hull, and ship again to Christiansand or Christiania. If so, it was the only time he ever set foot in England, the country he came to hate with a peculiar virulence.

The Second Visit, 1886–1888

No sooner had Hamsun arrived in Norway than he began to miss the United States. In retrospect, Elroy, Wisconsin, seemed to him an almost idyllic place, one where he had enjoyed the company of good friends and at least enough money to live on. Now he was lonely, friendless, still convalescing, and without a steady income. He could see only a dim prospect in his native land. Before the end of September 1884 he wrote to his friend Sven Tveraas, a farmer residing near Elroy, to say his present doctor had told him that if he lived until spring it would be all right for him to "travel back to America. And I think I will, if I live."

It was to be two years before he made the return voyage, though by the following spring he was not only alive but well enough to start on a lecture tour, speaking on various Scandinavian authors. He was not very successful, and he did no better when he repeated the effort in 1886. "The few who come are enthusiastic," he found, "but they are so few." Towns such as Horten and Sandefjord proved almost as disappointing as Stoughton had been.

Meanwhile Hamsun submitted "Letters from America" and other articles on American subjects to Christiania newspapers, which published a number of them. (He made the name Hamsun permanent after his essay on Mark Twain appeared in *Ny Illustrerte Tidende* on March 22, 1885, with a typographical error, the *d* having been omitted from Hamsund.) These newspaper articles reflected a disillusionment with American democracy, a certain disgust with American life, which did not dissuade him from returning to the United States. They brought him a little money, but not enough for him to avoid experiences like those of the starving would-be writer he was soon to describe in *Hunger*. "I ended up living a miserable life in Norway," he said after deciding to leave.

His reason for going was a little different from what it had been before. This time he intended not to make a name for himself in America but to prepare for a career in Norway. If he could make enough money to pay his debts and accumulate some savings, he would have the leisure to write when he came back. He hoped to earn the money as a roving reporter for two Christiania dailies. For his interim expenses, he relied again on his friends.

He embarked at Christiansand and, after a two-week voyage, landed at New York on September 3, 1886. Finding the 90-degree heat oppressive, he promptly took a train to Chicago. After arriving there, he wrote an account of the voyage that was published in *Dagbladet,* but he sent back no more such reports. Instead, he found a job on the street railways. At first he had to do heavy work with a maintenance and construction gang, but he was promised and was eventually given a coveted position as streetcar conductor. This paid what was then an excellent salary: $50 or $60 a month for a beginner, as much as $100 for an experienced employee. It was far more remunerative than writing articles. To suit his appearance to his new position, he had his hair cut short in the American style and began to grow a mustache.

Within a few years the street railways of Chicago and other cities would be electrified and trolley cars would be a familiar sight. As yet, horse- or mule-drawn cars were the rule, but cable cars were operating in some of the more up-to-date municipalities, among them Chicago. Hamsun described the system to a friend in Norway who had never seen such a modern wonder: "Let me tell you about it: they have trams here that go through the

streets by themselves—no horses, no engines—you just see a row of carriages coming toward you, and you can't see what it is that drives them
along. In fact, there's a thing under the ground that propels them, a cable
several English miles long, and in the road there is a slit where an arm con-
necting the carriages to the cable runs."

Aside from the fact that he worked for the streetcar company, little is
known about Hamsun's eight-month stay in Chicago. (Apparently he did
not associate much, if at all, with the Scandinavian literary circle there.) It
seems unlikely that he would have quit such a well-paying post, and possibly he was let go. Later stories raised questions about his job performance.
With his nearsightedness, it has been said, he had difficulty in making out
street signs so as to announce the stops, especially at night. He memorized
street names in the order of the stops, but if he missed one of the names he
would get all the rest wrong. His habit of reading as he rode presumably
added to his troubles. But these stories of his inattention and forgetfulness
may have arisen, at least in part, from his own ironic and self-belittling accounts to his friends.

Hamsun was back in Minneapolis by May 17, 1887, when he spoke at the
Syttende Mai (Norwegian Constitution Day) celebration in Dania Hall.
Again he had a rent-free room at the Jansons' house, and from time to time
he gave lectures on Scandinavian and other literature. He began to associate with a group of young Norwegian Christians who advocated a variety
of liberal causes.

The Jansons, as usual, left Minneapolis for the summer. Hamsun decided to move on west with a couple of friends in search of employment and
adventure. They went to Dakota Territory to look for railroad work but did
not like what they found and began to wander around in search of farm
work, sleeping in empty boxcars. One morning Hamsun shaved under the
bridge between Fargo, in the Dakota Territory, and Moorhead, Minnesota, which were on opposite sides of the Red River. "An old woman rinsing
clothes in the river stood watching and laughing at me," he wrote to Janson. "On the 4th of July we celebrated—there were three of us—as best we
could with a bottle of beer and a hunk of rye bread." Finally he obtained a
job on a "bonanza farm" near Casselton.

During the 1870s and 1880s the valley of the Red River, flat and fertile,
was covered with bonanza farms, so-called because of the fabulous profits

they yielded their proprietors, either corporations or individuals. These farms, measuring tens of thousands of acres and concentrating on the production of wheat, were highly mechanized. "Plows, drawn not by horses but by [steam] tractors, turn as many as twenty-two furrows at a time," Hamsun wrote. Mechanical reapers, horse-drawn, harvested the grain, and steam-powered machines threshed it. More than a thousand men were employed in a single operation, their work highly organized, with separate teams and foremen. The workday was long, fourteen to fifteen hours; the food unappetizing; the pay low. Most of the employees were immigrants, especially Scandinavians, desperate for a job. On such a farm, managed by Oliver Dalrymple, Hamsun labored during the summer and fall of 1887.

Returning to Minneapolis, he rented a room of his own, not because of any unfriendliness with the Jansons but because of a desire to be independent. During the winter he gave a series of talks on literary subjects, but he did not really like lecturing and was not making a living at it. His friends helped him get other jobs, such as pumping a church organ and taking care of a farmer's pigs, while he managed to sell a few articles. It was hard going most of the time.

By the spring of 1888 Hamsun was completely disillusioned with the "liberty" of which Americans boasted. He was wearing a black ribbon in sympathy with the four German immigrants who, as anarchists, had been sentenced to death—wrongly, he thought—for the 1886 Haymarket bombing in Chicago. Having decided to go home to Norway, he prepared a "farewell address" that he hoped would raise money for the trip. For two hours, on March 28, he harangued a full house in Dania Hall. This time his subject was not Norwegian literature but American culture, "and his point was that there was none of it," as a listener later said. He ridiculed American ways, even the standard greeting "How do you do?"—which, he pointed out, made no sense when translated literally into Norwegian ("Hvorledes gør du gør?"). He was forgetting that the standard greeting in Norwegian—"Hvordan staar det til?"—was equally meaningless in a literal English translation ("How stands it to?").

The speech failed to make enough money for his journey home, and again Hamsun had to depend on the generosity of friends. He stayed in Minneapolis long enough to speak at another Syttende Mai celebration, then departed, never to return to the United States.

America Remembered, 1889–1949

It has been said that Hamsun's anti-Americanism was one of the "elements" that "drove him into the arms of national socialism." Actually, his Anglophobia was far more extreme than his anti-Americanism, though the two were interrelated and mutually reinforcing. It was anti-Britishness more than anti-Americanism—and more than anti-Semitism—that made him a Nazi. His feelings toward the United States were complex and subject to change. They found expression in many of his writings: directly in his reminiscences and contemporaneous comments, indirectly in his fiction.

"I'm glad to be out of America," Hamsun wrote to a Minneapolis friend after leaving for the last time. While starving in Copenhagen, he wrote to another: "How pleased I am with this country. This is Europe, and I am a European—thank God!"

During the winter of 1889 he gave two lectures on America at the University of Copenhagen, elaborating on the strictures he had put forth in his Minneapolis farewell address. These he hastily elaborated further and published as his first important book, *On the Cultural Life of Modern America* (1889). In this diatribe he pictured the United States as a land of gross and greedy materialism, utterly lacking in literary and artistic originality or refinement. He also included personal recollections that suggest some of the sources of his resentment.

In particular, he was offended by the exaggerated patriotism of Americans, their continual boasting of themselves as the freest, most advanced, most intelligent people anywhere—boasting from which the foreigner could not escape. They even bragged about things that actually were European. "I had a sheath knife with a retractable blade that aroused a great deal of amazement; on a farm out in Dakota it was a much bigger hit than I was myself. 'Yeah, what will the damn Yankees think of next?' It took me a week to convince these people that the knife was a Swedish invention."

Americans claimed that their public schools were the best in the world, but the children were taught only about their own country and were left ignorant of foreign peoples and conditions, Hamsun complained. This ignorance permeated the population, the educated as well as the uneducated.

I have even found it among the teachers themselves. At the high school
in Elroy, Wis., there was in 1883 a teacher who was quite surprised when
I told him that we had the telegraph in Norway too—in 1883!—and he
used to look at the stamps on my letters from home in such a way that I
got the impression he did not believe his own eyes. "Do you also have a
postal system in Norway?" he asked. "This is 1883," I replied. The teacher,
like his pupils and his school, had got his knowledge of Norway from their
schoolbook, from four pages of a travel account by the American President Taylor, who had studied Norway from a rented horse cart in the
'fifties.

Hamsun himself was ill-informed. The account to which he referred was
written not by President Zachary Taylor but by the poet and travel writer
Bayard Taylor.

Americans knew so little about other countries and peoples, Hamsun
went on, that they called all Scandinavians Swedes. And "when a man is
called a Swede, it is in a disparaging way, as if he ought to apologize for being Swedish." It did no good for him to protest that he was not Swedish
but Danish or Norwegian. In fact, the Yankees looked down on all foreigners—except for one group.

To be Yankee-born is often a requirement for a worker to hold a job, especially one of the better positions in banks, public offices, and the railroad system. The only people who have the respect of the Americans, despite the national hatred following the War for Independence, are the
English. In England the United States sees a model and exemplar, and
remnants of old English civilization are still the latest fashion in modern
America. If you want to give a Yankee dude a compliment, take him for
an Englishman. He will lisp like the most honorable lord, and when he
rides the streetcar, he will give the conductor a gold piece or a large bill
to change.

This suggests that Hamsun's American experience contributed to his Anglophobia, despite his friendship with Americans of British background
such as Will Ager, Henry Johnston, and Harry Hart.

But the gravamen of Hamsun's complaint against the English was their
role as tourists in his country. He deplored the growth of tourism, viewing
it as a source of corruption and humiliation, a threat to Norway's national

character. Traveling in Norway, the "international Anglo-Saxons," including Americans, treated the people like curiosities and inferiors, he protested. In his books he depicted English tourists as ridiculous and contemptible creatures, sometimes going to positively sick extremes. Thus, in *The Last Joy* (1912), two visiting English characters engage in bestiality in a goat barn. "They had no regard for me, those two Englishmen in the goat barn. I was only one of the natives, a Norwegian, and I had to keep quiet about the mighty tourists. But they belonged to the nation of runners, wagon drivers, and vice, a nation whose wholesome fate will be for Germany one day to chasten it to death."

This was written just two years before the start of World War I. In that war Hamsun naturally favored the Germans, and he did so from the most patriotic of motives, though the great majority of his fellow countrymen disagreed with him. When the United States supplied and then joined the Allies, he acquired a new grievance against Americans and a confirmation of his old opinion of them. "Again and again," he wrote privately, "I find that the major criticism I made of Yankee materialism in that youthful book is confirmed by events." Germany's defeat he viewed as only a temporary setback.

During World War II the Nazis published a German edition of *On the Cultural Life of Modern America* as anti-American propaganda. While Hamsun expressed his views of the United States most fully in this book and in various articles, he also gave indirect and implied judgments in some of his fiction. Not that he set any of his novels in America or made any of his characters *born* Americans, but he depicted several of them as returning Norwegian emigrants, more or less Americanized.

Especially noteworthy is his character August, who figures in the trilogy that comprises *Vagabonds* (1927), *August* (1930), and *The Road Leads On* (1933). An orphan, August is rootless; he is a vagabond, a world seafarer, one who comes and goes. When he leaves the small arctic town of Polden, his close friend Edevart asks him if he is going back to America. "You need have no doubt about it," August replies. "There's no other part of the world for a man like me." After his departure, his friends agree among themselves that there is "Americanism" in him. Personally, he is appealing enough, a jokester and a fibber but helpful and unselfish, unconcerned with accumulating property for himself. He has constantly tried to industrialize and modernize the town, however, and some of his projects have either failed or, if successful, left the townspeople worse off than before.

Others among Hamsun's returning emigrants are quite different from August. Edevart, for instance, comes home dispirited, having been abandoned by his wife, who remains in America. Abel, a character in *The Ring Is Closed* (1936), is August's extreme opposite: unenterprising, ambitionless, constantly dreaming of his former life of ease in a subtropical paradise—as Hamsun described Kentucky, a state he had never been in.

But it is August who represents the America that Hamsun disliked—the America preoccupied with newness, mechanization, material progress. In the August novels and in other writings, including his Nobel Prize-winning *Growth of the Soil* (1917), he criticized explicitly or implicitly this trend toward modernization and cosmopolitanism while glorifying localism and life on the farm. Thus he espoused a conservative, anticapitalistic agrarianism of a kind that was captivating literary people elsewhere in Europe and in America. In the United States its most notable advocates were the Nashville Agrarians, with their manifesto *I'll Take My Stand* (1928). In Germany, Oswald Spengler and several prominent Nazis expressed similar ideas during the 1920s.

While locating none of his novels in the United States, Hamsun composed some shorter narratives about the American scene. These cannot be considered anti-American, though they do emphasize the strangeness, as the author saw it, of life in what he called Yankeeland.

The present collection brings together these and other scattered pieces, most of which have never been published, and none of which is readily available, in an English translation. They are arranged here in the order of their original publication, and they fall naturally into three categories:

1. Critical Reporting, 1885–1888. Articles appearing in Norwegian or Danish newspapers soon after each of Hamsun's visits in the United States and giving his views on a variety of American subjects.

2. Memory and Fantasy, 1897–1905. Narratives of life in America, most of which are presented as personal experiences but which actually are blends of fact and fiction.

3. Mellow Reminiscence, 1928 and 1949. Later and fonder recollections of experiences in the United States.

CRITICAL REPORTING
(1885–1888)

The American Character

Hamsun expressed his disillusionment with the United States in an article that was published in Aftenposten *(Christiania) on January 21, 1885, a few months after returning to Norway from his first American visit. In this essay he foreshadowed the strictures on American culture that he was later to develop much more fully, especially in* On the Cultural Life of Modern America *(1889).*

On the other side of the ocean lies a country as big as twenty kingdoms and incomparably rich—America, the Millionaires' Republic. People here in Norway are acquainted with it from geography lessons, America letters, and published lectures. I have been over there and have just come back. I went as a young man full of enthusiasm for the world's freest country and people, abounding in confidence that its society was sound. By the time I left, a few years later, my enthusiasm and my faith had been badly shaken. The same thing will happen to others. We live up here in the hills that rise like a second story above other European lands. Now and then the din carries up from down below, from the noisy, lively, lusty world. We feel the impact of the storm's exhilarating gust, and we are excitedly drawn along with it. This is the result of the America letters and the lectures. So we leave home—with preconceived notions and great expectations.

And we are often disappointed. Not in our hope of making money, for anybody can do that over there, nor in our appetite for a lot of food. No, our disappointment is strictly a matter of morality; it comes when our eyes are opened to the base, disreputable ways, the terrible abuse of what is legally permissible. We then get a sense of the danger that arises from the mixing of different kinds of people in a free, uncontrolled, capricious environment. The danger is all the greater in America, where shiploads of immigrants—diseased and degenerate human raw material—stream in every day from all over the world.

America's *principles* do not disappoint but are to be admired. Consider the idea that America should take the dregs of the European population and turn them into decent human beings. That in itself is not disappointing—that principle of humanity and freedom, the great and glorious sentiment that America can teach the rest of the world. The Declaration of Independence, upon which the laws and institutions of the United States rest, is one of the noblest documents of all history. It is the more remarkable in being the first of its kind, the first declaration in accordance with which a group of people has actually tried to *practice* independence, not only with respect to other countries but also among themselves. Public trust and equal rights—that is the basis on which America brings up its sons and daughters.

Such are the principles.

But the practice must here be emphasized. Life in America pulsates with greater emotional force and a more intensive use of power and means than elsewhere. When you have believed firmly in the ideal of an American social order and have expected happiness and well-being and contentment as a consequence, then—yes, that is when you are disappointed. The principles do not deliver what they promise.

The principles do not deliver what they promise! No, they remain, as ideals, too far from the reality of daily practice. I think there is a place for more real *living* humanity and conformity in a country based on American principles. But I think it takes a people more highly developed morally than the Americans to endure such free institutions and such immense wealth as theirs. And there is the especially frightful danger looming for the wide, magnificent West and for those who settle there. The time will come when they can no longer tolerate their freedom, and then America must restrain its people, thus altering its principles. Otherwise, if the flood of mean and sickly European immigrants persists, the nation must go to wrack and ruin. That is how it looks to me. Things cannot go on for very long the way they are now going. It is a historic impossibility for America, *with the same kind of citizens,* to survive as long as other nations.

Consider what *elections* are now like. I know what I have read in certain Norwegian newspapers about elections over there, but I also know how they operate in fact. Millions are spent on them, and that is why I call America the "Millionaires' Republic." Not only are individual votes bought but vote *buyers* are bought. These take on a particular job as a matter of business and receive their pay in cash. They buy posters to put up on walls and wagons on which the candidate's name is paraded in large letters. They even buy photographers, saloonkeepers, housewives, fathers and sons—and newspapers. Enormous sums are distributed to the newspapers before every election of any significance. They are paid to expand and to work in such-and-such a direction. And how do they work, these papers that live exclusively on this election money? They go to extremes that in any other country, with normal press freedom, would be considered criminal. Let us recall, as an example, what we have seen in the American press during the latest presidential election [between Grover Cleveland and James G. Blaine, 1884].

The Americans have *not* grown up and emerged safely from their country's history of freedom. For they are constantly being uprooted and broken up and mixed with the flood of European raw material and criminal elements. Who, among these fifty million, are really "Americans" and who are Irishmen, Scandinavians, Germans, Austrians? If Americans were today a single people who had been familiar with freedom and human rights from the beginning, and not a mixture of the most heterogeneous elements from all over the world, America would actually be what we ideally expect before we go there; it would be socially and morally as far ahead of other countries as it now is behind them. Though I believe it will take many years' development before any country can long endure with such free institutions, I nevertheless am confident that America can keep going for a while yet, especially if it puts a timely stop to immigration, or at least puts some restrictions on it.

I do not think liberty should be *liberties,* or well-being the only measure of success in life, but that is about what the Americans believe. It has been said that "as soon as you land in America you realize you are in a free country." This is said in praise of America, but what I saw was people taking liberties!

From the harbor I made my way up one of the busiest streets in New York. I was not used to such terrible traffic, which is due to the population density and the high cost of land, where there are buildings of sixteen stories, four of which lie below ground. Now, I saw one driver leave his wagon crosswise so as to unload into a warehouse, and another driver did the same on the other side of the street. These two blocked the passageway so completely that other drivers could not get by, and nine of them had to wait until one of the first two deigned to move.

I cannot help reporting another typical, everyday occurrence. A monster of a man raped a little girl right on the street in one of the large cities out West, but the fellow had connections who were about to get him acquitted. The moral sense of the community was aroused, and one fine night a mob with the *mayor himself* at the head of it stormed the city hall, took the prisoner out of his cell, and hanged him on a tree. See, when you have been in America for a while, you realize you are in a land of *liberties!* Such an evasion of law and order—when the imposition of justice seems so absolutely necessary—indicates a loose sense of law and morality. Here liberties were taken both by those who evaded the law and by those who ought to have enforced it. Even in cases where the law appears to have been properly enforced, a supplementary lynching often occurs, to demonstrate that you live in a free country.

No, I do not think that liberty consists of *liberties* or that well-being is the only measure of success in life. As soon as you land in America, you are put under strain at finding the rules of conduct so bewilderingly broad and people in such a nervous hurry. There are no limits to this eternal pursuit, from the time you are big enough to start work until the time you have to stop, and no limits to this nervousness about getting ahead as fast and as far as possible. The Americans are a restless, ambitious people. It is as if gigantic wheels were driving their whole existence with roaring speed. Once they hit upon an idea for getting ahead, they pursue it compulsively, working as hard as a slave, with boundless hope and great leaps of faith. People in other countries may be said to be engaged in a struggle for existence; here it must be called a struggle for *well-being*—for a kind of carnivorous, satiating existence, with the ability to afford intense sensual pleasures along with fat horses and rich food. The typical American has no real artistic sense or substantial literary, religious, political, or social interests. Consequently, when he is forty or fifty and has accumulated enough to be free from care for the rest of his life, he no longer craves so much what used to seem like necessities, and his zest for life is satiated—if not vitiated. So overworked as he is, the American can hold out only so long and then must stop.

Yet, in sheer material terms, the Americans are livelier than any other people, as is shown by their powers of invention, boldness of enterprise, and rage for speculation—what might be called their *machinelust*. This results from the *positive* side of the population mixture, besides the country's natural conditions. From the beginning the people have been surrounded by machines, ingenious contrivances to lighten their toil and yield them the greatest possible profit. From childhood they have been familiar with railroad trains roaring by, as well as machines that mow, trim, rake, wash, knit, dry, hoist, plane, etc.

And with machines they manufacture the largest, the smallest, the most amazing things. I have eaten a hen's egg from a Brooklyn *egg factory*, where not only the yolk but even the thin membrane between the white and the shell were placed where they belong. Nothing was lacking. In some of the large Eastern cities I have seen jugglers' machines with which they swindle people who take a chance on a number. These machines, nicely made of polished steel, contain whirring little wheels, weblike strings, and hidden works. It must be added that America also provides Europe with its best instruments for dentists, midwives, and hospitals. Indeed, when it comes to applied science or technology, the United States is ahead of all other countries, even those where fine mechanisms are a specialty— Switzerland, for example.

But this special distinction of the Americans is marred by their propensity for boundless speculation. With their technical ability they are insatiable in their craving for newer, always newer things. They plan, make rough estimates, fool with tremendous projects, get excited about the wildest impossibilities—and often ruin themselves in the process. But they do not give up. They suffer from a national mania, an incurable disease, one that keeps on spreading. Onward, onward! is the eternal cry, and onward they go eagerly, greedily.

An example: In New York City, where there is neither coal gas nor petroleum gas, a practical American—and all Americans are "practical"—recently made an interesting experiment to produce gas from street refuse. The attempt succeeded brilliantly, seventeen ounces of trash yielding twenty-two cubic feet of gas at little cost. Formerly the city's ashes and garbage were transported several miles out to sea, but the incoming tide carried rotten eggs, cabbages, and dead cats back to the beaches, thus driving hotel owners crazy. Now their torment was over. Now the dead cats would be converted into gas!

Hardly had this experiment been reported in the *New York Herald* when another practical American conceived an even more original plan: He was going to make gas out of the city's *corpses.* New York having a population of 1.5 million, he could count on sixty to seventy thousand deaths per year. Just think of the gas from all these! It would double the city's "well-being." Seventy thousand corpses—how delightful such statistics! That is the way the Americans' brains operate.

Their brains keep going tirelessly and with the passion of a serious gambler. Many of the Americans "work their way up," as they say over there, from tenant farmer's son to property owner; from riverboat oarsman to the country's highest honor, the presidency; from a little warehouse job to railroad king; from selling matches on the street to millionaire. Jay Gould, the great railroad prince of the East, told a U.S. Senate committee that, when he was fourteen years old, he had to leave home without a cent. Two years after that he had $500; soon, with a successful speculation in map-making, $5,000; and a few years later, with the purchase and sale of a mill, $50,000. Then he became the owner of the Rutland & Washington line and, not long after that, the Cleveland & Pittsburgh, while borrowing money and buying stocks at low prices. Next, he invested $5 million in the Union Pacific, bought and sold other railroads, developed coal mines, and made enormous amounts of money. Now, after forty years, he is one of the four men in the United States whose millions secretly run the country.

Such are American captains of industry, but some exhibit even more boldness and energy. Enterprises do not always depend on careful planning and calculating, but quite often are merely the result of a brilliant flash of madness. A [Wisconsin] acquaintance told me: "I bet on trotting horses; that's my profession. I have bet and made a bundle one day and lost everything the next. One year I went down to Chicago with $10,000; when I came home I was so completely wiped out that I had to work in a mill all the following summer. The next winter I went back and won $35,000 on five bets. I'll never be broke again; nowadays I only risk half of what I own—that's enough." An American can stand to lose his money. He does not get sick, nor does he poison or shoot himself, like the more delicate European. A New Yorker is still alive who last winter lost his immense fortune speculating in railroad lands. At present he has a job as a clerk in a branch office, but he will try again! If you think he is going to give up, you are mistaken. An American is not cut out that way.

New York City

Though he had spent only a few days in New York City, Hamsun chose to write about it rather than about Elroy, Wisconsin, where he had lived for nearly two years. He no doubt assumed that Norwegian newspaper readers would be more interested in the metropolis. For sources, he depended not only on his personal observations but also on conversations with New Yorkers, on the city's newspapers, and on various encyclopedic references. This essay appeared in two installments in Aftenposten *on February 12 and 14, 1885.*

*T*wo centuries ago the little island of Manhattan, the site of present-day New York, was bought from the Indians for twenty-four dollars (eighty-five Norwegian kroner). In 1643 the first lots were divided among Dutch colonists, the earliest of whom, Martin Krieger, obtained the place where the colossal Trinity Church now stands, and where the city's most magnificent buildings are located, on Broadway and Wall Street. His only neighbors at that time were wild animals and Indians, whose attacks he had to be constantly prepared for. It is different now. The island, twenty-five kilometers long and three wide, is estimated to be worth $610 million for the land alone, while the mansions, churches, hotels, city hall, and post office amount to about twice as much.

An Irishman, who came to New York and started out with a small grocery business, is now "worth" $25 million and lives in an elegant little castle. The metropolitan newspaper *New York Herald* also "lives" here in an immensely valuable marble palace. There are department stores that pay an annual rent of $20,000 to $80,000, and hotels whose sumptuous luxury has become a byword in every country. One of these splendid buildings is Stewart's great fancy-goods emporium, the owner of which has a fortune of several million dollars. A mile away are some quite ordinary-looking two-story buildings valued at $200,000 each and renting for $2,000 to $10,000 a year. Here also is a cluster of marble hotels: Delmonico's, the Albemarle, the Golden House, Hoffmann's, the St. James, and O'Boyle's House, among others. The stretch of fine houses continues all the way to Central Park, which is said to be even more beautiful than the Bois de Boulogne. The Indians could not get all this back for the eighty-five kroner they sold it for two hundred years ago.

At the last census (1880) New York contained 1,206,590 souls (about 300,000 more than ten years earlier), 611,295 of them women and 595,295 men, 723,597 of them unmarried. None of these people produce their own food. They even get their drinking water from a distance, 66 million gallons a day, flowing through enormous pipes from the Croton Reservoir forty miles away. These waterworks have cost no less than $30 million, the city paying annually $1 million in direct expenses and $2 million for interest on the borrowed capital. You see, it costs money to quench your thirst in New York, even if you do it with water.

Especially with ice water. The sale of ice is in the hands of ten or a dozen large companies, which have constructed storehouses holding as much as 620,000 tons of ice each. At a price of three or four cents a pound, people will have to pay a lot if they want *cold* water.

Not to mention stronger beverages. Americans are for temperance, it is said, and it is true. Yet there are more than a hundred thousand people in the United States who are employed in the manufacture and sale of alcoholic drinks. According to the 1880 census, there are 16,278 brewers and maltsters, 3,245 distillers, 68,461 saloonkeepers and bartenders, and 13,500 dealers in wine and other intoxicating beverages. In New York itself there are between eight and ten thousand drinking places, where all kinds of such beverages are available. It is quite incredible how much alcohol New Yorkers consume every year. About 350 million gallons of domestic whiskey are brought in, and to this quantity must be added what the city itself produces and what is imported from Europe. It all goes to show that, if New York lacks anything, it is not the means to slake your thirst. The United States as a whole imports $10 million worth of spirits from Europe, but this sum would be cut by one-third if there were a million fewer Irishmen in the country.

The city gets its fish, meat, and grain from Illinois, Minnesota, Maryland, Wisconsin, Tennessee, and Missouri. From these sources come annually about five million sacks of flour and nine million bushels of grain. New Jersey provides wild fowl, Maine trout, Iowa poultry, Vermont mutton, Savannah anchovies, the Chesapeake oysters, Kansas pork, Texas beef, and Nebraska eggs, while all thirty-six [actually thirty-eight] states supply apples and other fruits. For all this, the expense adds up to an enormous sum. The consumption of luxury foods alone, so far as New York City is concerned, amounts to $600,000 a year. New Yorkers are not content with just what the United States can provide. Besides the railroads running in with their tremendous loads from the Kennebec River and from the Colorado mountains, there are the countless sloops and schooners that busily ply the coast with cargoes bound for New York. From Bermuda they come loaded with potatoes, from Newfoundland with fish, from Turkey with plums, from Smyrna with figs, from Cuba with oranges, and from all the Mediterranean countries with tropical fruits. The Erie Canal flotilla unloads its riches, and the Hudson River's broad surface can hardly accommodate all the vessels that force their way toward New York.

The city has an absolutely first-rate location for commerce, and with the exception of London there is no place with shipping of greater importance. The Hudson and East rivers and the Erie and Delaware canals, together with the numerous rail lines, all empty into New York carrying the natural products of the United States. In reality, the city does not consist of Manhattan alone but stretches out to a diameter of thirty-five to forty miles, and its population should be supplemented by the 566,689 in Brooklyn, besides about a half-million uncounted transients, probably the largest number anywhere in the world.

Businessmen, of course, form the most powerful class in New York. Three of the largest manufacturing firms annually realize $8 million apiece from the sale of their products. Most numerous are the wine and brandy dealers; after them come grocers, then bakers, next butchers, and finally confectioners. Lawyers number about 2,300, brokers of all kinds 1,600, physicians 1,200 to 1,300, and druggists 500 to 600. The tailors are 50,000 strong and the shoemakers about twice as numerous. There is an equal number of clergymen and wig makers, 500 to 600, and double that number of cigar dealers, 1,200.

There are two other groups that must not be passed over in silence. It is estimated that 2,500 are thieves by profession, who of course live as best they can, some of them becoming quite wealthy. They form regular companies, in which they occupy different levels, ranging from the ragged tramp on the country roads to the elegant "gentlemen" who carry on their business in the finest hotels. These men never steal from women but leave that to their brethren of a lower order. In this kind of life, too, there is opportunity to "work your way up." A couple of rich men in New York, for example, worked their way up from rank to rank, from tramps to gentlemen. Now, having retired from the business, they live off their fortunes, which are rumored to be $500,000 each, not counting the small castles they occupy. The other class consists of the fallen women. Of these, the police have knowledge of only 5,000 at most, but people who have been around a bit in New York, and who have had an opportunity to add up the numbers in certain areas, are convinced that the total for the entire city must be much higher—30,000.

A large sum, about $4.6 million a year, is spent on police, jails, and reformatories. Drink, drink—that is what, here as elsewhere, accounts for much of the expense of law enforcement. A fourth of the people the police arrest are intoxicated, and half of these are Irishmen. New York unfortunately gets its share of the criminals and riffraff among the immigrants from the Old World, who significantly reinforce the strength of the native-born scoundrels. The city maintains a uniformed police force of 2,500 men, besides a number of plainclothes detectives, to keep the lawbreakers in check. But these individuals have the same rights as law-abiding citizens, and on election days they troop up to the polls along with respectable people and receive cash for their vote. This lack of moral sense is the harmful aspect of the general liberality of American institutions.

To New York come all kinds—speculators, fortune hunters, gamblers, murderers—all who know one "business" or another. They come to ply their old trades or to find new ones. Wild and feverish commotion ensues, with brilliant success or ruinous failure, for the temptations are irresistible, the consequences often amazing. Men set their sights high and defy all odds. New York is an enormous marketplace, a permanent fair, a bazaar without boundaries, where all the Union's and all the world's buyers and sellers meet. This continual nervous activity has become the earmark of the city, and it has left its distinctive impress upon the inhabitants themselves. An experienced observer can tell a New Yorker from a Westerner even without hearing the difference in the way they talk. The New Yorker's kind of activity has made him more alert, smarter, than Western people. You do not find lazy men in New York; the lazy ones soon become discouraged and go back to their homelands or move farther into the interior of the States.

You see what the New Yorker is like as soon as you land. For example, he does not take his hat off. I came from good old Europe, where a man when recognized on the street must carry his hat in his hand. From the time he sees an acquaintance approaching in the distance until he meets him, he calculates how many steps he has left before he must remove his hat or his cap, which hand he is going to use, and how deep and how long he ought to bow. I came from good old elegant Europe, where even after death a ranking order is observed between the blessed and the highly blessed, the most blessed and the most highly blessed. In New York a person gets absolutely no respect—everybody is simply too busy. A man walks brazenly past and greets you in a loud voice: "How do you do?" On Karl Johan Street [in Christiania] you would speak that way only to somebody whose company you did not desire. In New York an acquaintance passing by will usually ask how you are ("How do you do?") without bothering to wait for an answer. He does not have time.

A lady whom I passed on a New York street, and who knew I was a foreigner and thus unacquainted with the rights of women in a modern city, gently made me aware that they *always* had a right to the inside of the sidewalk. Unlike her, the ladies in Europe would be properly silent. In Brooklyn another lady—I guess I can call her a "lady"—said to me, "You don't know much," because I could not tell her where the New York post office was. So much for American friendliness on the street! Be quick and go on past. God bless you—you do not have time to stop.

That is what New Yorkers are like, always on the go, always trying to get ahead of one another. And they do it all with a kind of dignity. They dress well, live high if sometimes wildly, and do not flinch from the most foolhardy speculations. If they fall, they get up again; even among the successful there are few who have not experienced a reversal of fortune a couple of times. They love beautiful houses, splendid furniture, and exceptional racehorses. The women are like the men—attractive, elegant, stylish, ambitious, a bit prudish. They are brilliantly groomed and dressed, with jewels and lace, and they can live "like people" *only* between Fourth and Sixth avenues and Union Square and Central Park. A woman in this circle has nothing to do except to spend money. She has no occupation, no duties, and no cares—except to care about herself, her nerves, her cramps, her rouged and powdered face, and her ambitious plans, which worry her more than anything else.

The cultivated class, or "society," as it is called here, changes continually, like a kaleidoscope. No longer to be seen are the faces you knew and were fond of five or ten years ago. A few ghosts from the past may still wander around, but the fashion leaders are gone—nobody knows where and nobody asks. New York is much too busy, much too feverishly active, to waste time on useless sentimentality. Nobody recognizes his neighbor after the man goes broke or is arrested for some swindle; in either case the acquaintanceship comes to an end. Presidents of the United States are highly desirable as guests in the houses of the wealthy for four or at most eight years, that is, during their term of office. But when that is over, so is their desirability, unless they happen to be wealthy themselves, in which case they continue to belong to "society," like other rich men. Marriage becomes more and more difficult when young girls are used to complete indolence regarding everything but affairs and amusement.

New Yorkers know little about literature or art. In society you hear great old names bandied about amid the rustle of silk: Shakespeare, Doré, Ole Bull, Longfellow, Christina Nilsson, etc. This reflects the romantic view, which, after becoming antiquated in Europe, remains quite serviceable in New York. New Yorkers do not recognize the one native modern poet, Walt Whitman, a genius of considerable importance. He is "coarse." In American literature there have to be moonlight and singing birds and love affairs, but no questioning, no discussion, no catharsis; everything must end in such a way that they "get each other." Christopher Janson, who usually arranges for them to "get each other" at the very end, told me he recently had offered a story without a happy ending to *Harpers' Monthly* but got it back with the comment that it was "too painful." This typifies the trend of art criticism over there. They present Longfellow as *their* poet—with his hum, his lulling rhythms, his images of trees (not forests), bridges over rippling sky-blue brooks, stars—and of course moonlight. I remember the following:

> The day is cold, and dark, and dreary;
> It rains, and the wind is never weary.
> The vine still clings to the moldering wall,
> But at every gust the dead leaves fall.

A bit of melancholy in a nice little verse. By Longfellow. He was a significant writer with a rich versifying fluency and a *pure* outlook on life. But he became a *poet* mainly by virtue of the fact that he succeeded in representing the whole of romantic poetry to the people who in more ways than one are the greatest on the planet. I shall later deal more fully with American literature in comparison with contemporary literature. I say "contemporary" as distinct from American to suggest my conception of what is special about American writing.

Theaters, concert halls, and other places of entertainment are heavily patronized in New York. Barnum lives there with all his animals and strange humans, and Lady Christina still wins honors there. During the summer, when she toured from New York to San Francisco, she got a storm of applause at every stop. Now, I would not say her voice has been strained; I dare not even whisper that her voice is cracked. New Yorkers spend $8 million to $10 million a year on shows of all kinds. It is a terrible waste of money, since the level of dramatic art is so low that even "Professor" Hjalmar Hjort Boyesen can get his "dramatic" drivel presented.

Much better spent was the money that went into the construction of Central Park. It cost $10 million, but this converted a bare place into a miraculous garden with fountains, marble naiads, flowering hills, a sea of fragrant plants, and music every Saturday afternoon that attracts a tremendous crowd.

In New York you find a great many libraries, both public and private. The most important is Astor's, but the most visited is the Commercial Library, which contains 56,000 volumes.

There are approximately three hundred schools, which cost the city about $3 million a year. In all these schools the instruction is quite respectable, and in the largest it even includes dead languages. The teaching method also is excellent, discipline being maintained and science subjects accurately taught even in the smallest schools. It is a telling fact that thousands of academics offer to teach at a lower wage than even the youngest journeyman bricklayer gets. In America, too, the aversion to unskilled labor has become so great that "nice" jobs are taken even at a sacrifice.

The so-called "independent" professions, however, pay fairly well. Some lawyers, after years of strenuous effort, work their way up to an annual income of $50,000, while others make from $5,000 to $20,000, and still others as little as $2,000 to $4,000. Doctors earn about the same as lawyers. Clergymen get from $2,000 to $10,000.

But the great majority of workers must make do with much less. The average wage amounts to less than $400 a year (about 1,200 to 1,300 Norwegian kroner). That is not much in New York. The majority live in overcrowded, unhealthful tenements, where half the children die before they reach the age of five. Of the city's 160,000 families (in 1860), 15,000 included the enormously rich who had an entire house to themselves; the rest were crammed into buildings that contained an average of seven families each. It is reckoned that 15,000 to 20,000 others make up the underground population, living in cellars. All together, the poor are estimated to number as many as 60,000.

Let us walk down Cherry Street on a winter evening. Damp cellars, each occupied by five to seven families. Men, women, and children lying around in a room without fire, without beds, with nothing but piles of straw under them. Here live those with no chance of rising in society, with pale, starved faces, without friends, without hope. We should not judge too harshly the unfortunates, living in such conditions, who are driven to secure a livelihood for themselves and theirs by whatever means they can.

One evening, just as I was about to turn back to the hotel, I saw an old man ahead of me on Cherry Street who particularly attracted my attention. He was extremely ill-clad for the cold weather, and when I overtook him and got a closer look at him I could see the most obvious signs of malnutrition. He nevertheless had fine features and a quite intelligent face.

"Good evening, sir," he greeted me. "It sure is cold."

"Very cold," I replied. "It's a time to be warmly dressed, I suppose."

"Yes," he remarked, "for those who are not used to being cold."

"Are you used to being cold, you poor fellow?" I asked. I really did not like the man. There was a tightness around his lips, as if he were repressing a great deal of pain, of hard physical suffering. I pitied him more than I can say.

"Well, yes, I have finally managed to get used to it," he answered, "more so than I ever thought I would." A warm, almost red smile appeared on his blue mouth. "At one time I had all the clothes I needed," he went on, "but then things went downhill."

He proceeded to tell me he had made an invention and it had brought him to ruin—a large-print psalmbook for the elderly, with *electric* letters that could be read in the dark. For seven years he had worked on this invention, experimented, employed printers, and applied for a patent, but the thing was never quite perfected—he did not yet have the right kind of glow in the letters—though he was confident that it would eventually be a success. For the time being, he was so utterly ruined that it seemed almost impossible for him to get on his feet again. Wife and children, sir! Many children.

What did he do now to pay for food for them?

"Now? I work in a planing mill, sir," he answered. "That's where my clothes get torn up this way, with me carrying planks to the workbench. But that means nothing to me. After all, I'm an old man." And then he smiled again.

I could not stand it any longer. This needy man who did not beg or complain or bother strangers any more than absolutely necessary with his personal affairs—I could not just push him away. We had now come to an intersection. The man courteously bade me good-night and was about to go down a cross street to the left.

"No, wait a bit," I said. "Let's go in here and get you a wool jacket or an overcoat. You must be colder than is good for you—in those rags."

We went into a clothing store and got a warm wool jacket, which I had practically to force the fellow to put on. I stuck a little money in its pocket. Shedding a tear, he thanked me as if I had saved his life, and indeed I had the self-satisfied feeling of having just rescued someone.

I continued on my way down dark, narrow streets, where only a few of the gaslights were lit and there was no traffic. Just as I was about to turn up toward one of the main streets, I saw a man come out of a shop. In the glow of a nearby gaslight I quickly recognized him: it was the man with that wool jacket on. He went right in front of me and walked rather fast for two or three minutes. Suddenly he bent over, as if he had found something in the street, and, sure enough, when I caught up with him he was holding up a ring and looking at me.

"You're lucky now," I said as I examined the ring, which appeared to be of thick gold with carat marks and a good-looking white stone. "You will get a nice reward for this."

"Lucky?" he said. "No, I'm not lucky. You're a stranger here and don't know the laws. I'd have to spend all day tomorrow with interrogation and the calling of witnesses if I took this ring to the police station and said I had found it. And I can't be away from the planing mill for a single day. For one thing, I would probably lose my job; hundreds of men would be looking for it. For another thing, I've got to have tomorrow's wages to live on. I have a family, many children, sir, many small children."

"What are you going to do, then?" I asked. "You can't very well keep it, can you?"

"No, it would not clothe me very well," he replied, smiling and drawing attention to his ragged garb. "If I were to wear this ring tomorrow, I would be hauled into court and convicted of theft, regardless of the fact that I did not steal it. That's the way it is here when a man isn't rich enough to pay the jury to acquit him."

"But, my dear fellow, what shall we do, then?" I asked, sympathizing with the man.

"Now, you must not be annoyed with me, sir, but I must beg you to be so kind as to take the ring and hand it over to the police. That way, I can avoid losing my place at the planing mill, and I will gladly give up any claim to the reward. If you will be so kind—so helpful."

Well, I had little desire to be subjected to interrogation on account of a ring found on the street in New York, its owner unknown. Nor was I crazy about the idea of being held all of tomorrow by the police, when I had other plans for the day. I told the man that I did not want the assignment.

"No, I shouldn't have expected you to. I sincerely beg your pardon, sir! But then I have no idea what to do—none at all. I have a daughter at home who would be glad to have the ring, a pretty daughter, sir, sixteen years old. But what she needs, the poor thing, is food—food, not jewelry. Poor Clara!" Here he paused for a moment. "But now I know what," he resumed, his eyes brightening. "I can leave it where I found it." With that, he made as if to throw it back in the street.

"No, wait now!" I cried. "Wait a minute. So you have a daughter at home who is going hungry—a sweet young daughter? And her name is Clara, and she is good to her little brothers and sisters? And you can't afford enough food for her?"

"Unfortunately—" he began.

"Here's two silver dollars," I said. "If the ring is worth more, you'll get the rest tomorrow evening. Come to the Hotel Lincoln." Then we parted. I stuck the ring in my vest pocket.

I saved myself the trouble of going to a jeweler and selling the ring. The next morning I quickly discovered that the brightest thing about a "gold ring" you give money for on a New York street is the glass stone, which does not rust. The man never came to the Hotel Lincoln. I am now convinced that he had the ring in his hand when he bent over as if to pick it up, that he had bought it in the shop I saw him come out of. He was a greater psychologist than I; he certainly had my number. I wish him the best of luck with his electric psalmbook!

This incident exemplifies the neediness and the swindling ways of the inhabitants of Cherry Street. But among the New Yorkers, in addition to the wealthy, there is also the great majority of decent, steady laborers who work hard and earn a living honestly. More than 125,000 are employed in the city's factories, many of them processing raw materials from elsewhere in the United States. Go from Broadway along the cross streets and along the banks of the Hudson and the East River, and you will hear the din of hammers and saws, the groan of mighty machines, the whir of enormous wheels and rollers—the ceaseless activity of thousands of mechanical contrivances.

Yellow Thunder's Camp

Two years after visiting the Indian camp with his "teacher friend" Will Ager,
Hamsun saw his account of the experience published in Aftenposten *in two in-*
stallments, May 2 and 4, 1885. In the meantime he apparently had forgotten a
few key facts. The tribe consisted of Winnebagos, not Shawnees, and the chief was
not the great Yellow Thunder (who had died in 1874) but his son of the same
name. In his attitude toward the chief's son-in-law, Broad Shoulders, Hamsun
shows his fascination with the conflict between nature and culture, a theme that
was to reappear in some of his later writings.

When I heard that an Indian tribe had camped not far from Briggsville,
[Wisconsin,] the town where my teacher friend lived, I decided to go over
to the camp and try to get into it. This is something the pure-blooded
Shawnees would rather not permit, but I relied on my friend. He not only
could speak the Indian language a little but was personally acquainted with
one of the chief's sons, with whom he had often gone hunting. He also had
met the chief himself a couple of times.

My friend and I made our way out to the camp. While still some distance from it, we could hear the noise of many people and of dogs and don-
keys, and by the time we reached the outer tepees the din began to bother
us. A flock of Indian children with runny noses and bare bodies met us. Not
for a long time had they seen anything so interesting as my friend and me—
to judge by their gaping and gesturing.

We motioned one of the young Indians to us, one who was naked except
for a blanket over his shoulders. My friend asked him which was the chief's
tepee. Farther on. We now went past a row of tepees and finally came to
one that, by its larger size and better construction, could be recognized as

the chief's. Colored ribbons were fluttering at the entrance; from inside came the sound of bells and hoarse flutes and the voices of women singing. We asked some children outside whether they thought the chief would open his tepee for us travelers, who "wanted to see the breadth of his chest and hear the august sound of his voice." At the instigation of the children two warriors came out, one of whom was my friend's acquaintance, the chief's son. On behalf of the chief, they wanted to know whether we had brought firewater with us—if so, it must be deposited outside—and whether we intended to spend the whole night in the chief's tepee. Neither the one nor the other, we replied. So we could go in. As we were about to enter, though, there was a hasty counterorder. The chief wanted us to wait outside the tepee for a little while; inside were naked women who must first cover themselves up. Finally there came the go-ahead signal and we stepped in.

In the middle of the tepee a fire of twigs was burning, and women were stretched out around it. Animal skins were spread out along the edges. On one of them, a gem-studded elk hide, the chief was leaning lazily on an elbow, his eyes tired, half-closed. Suddenly he awoke, sat upright, and gave a nod of recognition to my friend, while seeming not to notice me. Yellow Thunder was a big, heavyset Indian with sharply cut brown features and a severe look. His costume was like the others', though perhaps a bit richer, and his head-feather was thicker and glossier. Yellow Thunder was a tame savage who spoke English fairly well and knew something of the white man's way of life. The savage in him was a trait he inherited from the tribe, which had chosen him as its leader on the warpath and the buffalo hunt. His painted face was beautiful in its wildness. He was a skillful spy and a chief of boundless courage. Once, in the time of President Pierce, he led a revolt against the United States Army, and he would not give up until the government promised him both his life and his tribe. Such was Yellow Thunder.

His wife was a rather short, heavy-limbed Indian woman from a hunting tribe out in Wyoming. They had two daughters and two sons. One of the daughters had been married to a French-Indian half-breed, whose story was connected with the peculiar question that the chief had put to us: whether we had any firewater.

"His mother was White River-Flower," Yellow Thunder related, "who went along with her father on the warpath and over the broad hunting fields. One summer a French artist came to her father's camp and wanted to paint White River-Flower's portrait on canvas. At that time she was as beautiful as a doe trembling in the hills and as quick in her dance as when the autumn lightning bares itself on its bed of clouds. She was slender as a soft sea wave, and her smile was like the rising sun. She allowed herself to be painted by the French stranger and, willingly enough, allowed herself to rest in his arms in the evenings after he finished. But when, one evening, *he* wanted to rest in *her* arms, she wriggled free and fled. Two days later the painter reappeared—with firewater. An Indian *must* drink firewater when it is offered; he becomes excited as soon as he smells it, and it is easier for him to stand before the muzzle of a cocked gun than to let firewater go once it is served. The whole tepee got drunk, White River-Flower too. Befuddled and exhausted, she sank back on the deerskin; and when darkness spread like a veil and everyone in the tepee was asleep, the painter, greedy with lust, sneaked over to White River-Flower's couch. The next spring she gave birth to a child and then died. So it went with White River-Flower, and her fate is that of many Indian girls. Conscienceless traveling white men dupe our young girls with firewater and destroy their youth."

We listened to the chief's account with great interest. His voice was hollow but powerful and rather agreeable. He said the quality of his voice was given him by the Great Spirit during a battle. Did we want to listen some more to the booming of his voice and learn how the story came out? He resumed:

"White River-Flower's child fell into the hands of white people, who suspected the tribe of having kidnapped him. For the boy was as fair as a freshly blooming morning glory, and his form was as supple as a forest lily's tender stem. The child remained among white folk until he became a young man; he got to know the white folk's learning and customs, and he went on the deer hunt with the white man's firearms. His relatives in the tribe knew where he was staying, and they saw his mind being turned to the white man's way, but they left him untouched in the woods and on the mountains. More and more he longed for the wide plains and the buffalo herds. Finally his yearning drew him away from the white man's home and over the wild mountains and the murmuring creeks. Then he found us, learned our language, and married my daughter. We call him Broad Shoulders."

There, in the opening of the tepee, he stood, broad-shouldered indeed and with his chest defiantly outthrust. His eyes, dark, irresistible, consumed us. His neck was thick, his hair abundant, and his face a warm, healthy brown. He was dressed in trousers and vest but had an Indian blanket over his shoulders and moccasins on his feet. He was beautiful. Experience tells us that disproportions result from the crossing of the wild, primitive, and copper-hued with the tame, civilized, and pale. The offspring gets all of the primitive race's hot, uncontrolled wildness without any of the cultured soul's powers of self-limitation. He inherits the civilized parent's sickliness and organic inferiorities, becomes round-shouldered and hollow-chested, has weak legs, a rough-hewn forehead, and a misshapen nose. But Broad Shoulders had no visible defects. His skin was merely a darker paleness than the white man's, and his nose but slightly bent in the direction of the Hebraic. His solid body swung on a pair of legs that would never have shaken or slipped, and he offered his chest to whoever had the courage to shoot at it. Thus he stood in the opening of the tepee.

My friend spoke to him in English; he listened for a second as if reflecting, then bowed to us in the Indian manner and sat down with us. Of the conversation between my friend and Broad Shoulders,[1] I here quote the most essential points:

"When do you intend to return to the white man?"

"Oh, never!" he answered. "Never! I am tired of the restlessness of civilized life. I have lived it for twenty summers and have come to know its rituals and cold cunning. I pained my soul with its algebra and its etymologies, and I learned to walk with the correct eighteen-inch step. But I

---

1. This Broad Shoulders, whom I met here, is an actual person; his name as a United States citizen is Louis Newman. As the Indian Chief Yellow Thunder correctly tells, he was brought up by the whites, who always thought he had been kidnapped by the Indians. The young Louis received a good education from the very beginning. He showed such eagerness for book learning that he was sent to the town's (Boise City's) high school. Here he graduated with a good record and then went to a larger high school, where he also graduated. After that, he went back home and entered the town's seminary. During his stay at this institution he often contributed articles to the town's newspapers, while he also, upon request, gave several public lectures on cultural subjects. Civilization became too confining for him, however, so one fine day he left home and never afterward could be persuaded to return. His conversation with my friend is accurately reported, since I was in a position inside the tepee to record it in all its peculiarities while it went on.

suffered, suffered in that palsied life; my breath dried up and my ambition wasted away in my breast. Then I fled."

"And you have never longed to go back?"

"Yes, yes, many a day and many a night, for I was so unfortunate as to be trained in the white man's strict ways. I missed his language, his books, his bedding, his plates. But out on these wild plains, where the buffalo hordes bellow, the prairie wind roars like an avalanche, and the warrior storms an enemy tribe to avenge a little wrong—here a man forgets the tame whites. Here he forgets the white man's cultured paragraphs and all his science and all his brain-breaking."

"But can one entirely forget the society one has been associated with, the society of civilized humans, the only true humans?"

Broad Shoulders acted as if hurt by this question. He promptly stood up, threw the blanket in full folds around his shoulders, and replied—with a warm blush on his forehead:

"If you had asked me what I call 'true humans,' I would not have answered that it was these weak, windblown whites who go around trembling like dry straw in the breeze, or that it was those who walk about with degenerate limbs and with water in their veins—the clever, civilized humans. I would have said *these* are an inferior species of the 'real' humans, their whole life is a constant sick health, their frantic striving a decadent activity—like that of flies in autumn—and all their knowledge merely boastful smoke. But if you had asked me who the 'real humans' were, I would have answered: the natural people, the aborigines!"

"Sit down, eager young son of the forest, sit down. You captivate me with your command of the language and your wonderful truths. And you did not get them on your own. You have been exposed to them at some time in your life? You have gone to school?"

"I have been exposed to them and have gone to school," Broad Shoulders replied. "Yes, I have gone to school: to high school and to the seminary in Boise City, Idaho. I can be considered a 'real human' despite the marks of the red race that I bear. Yes, I have gone to school and studied the dead books. I read for a degree like a madman—like a white person. All my days were taken up with exhausting concentration on the pages of a book; my nights were filled with anxiety and unhealthy sleep. For I was an Indian and had my race's hot temperament and its aspirations. I could not stand the effect of all the knowledge that buzzed in my brain. I came to have the cunning, watchful, cautious attitude that Indians get when they are civilized, and my proud back stiffened in an upright position; but I acquired sunken lungs and the white man's delicate nervousness. I would get up three times during the night to see if the door was locked. And my white sister, who used to go deer hunting with me every fall and hover around me like a fluttering bird in the woods—when she grew up she forgot her dark brother and disowned me in the eyes of the world."

"And that's why you ran away, Broad Shoulders?"

"That's why. Because I couldn't live in the will-breaking discipline of civilization; because its contrariness, tyranny, and violence wearied me, plagued me in my inmost soul. Its education, its knowledge, drained my brain, and after all the instruction I felt a painful withering, as the spring growth on a soft field must feel when wheel tracks cut through it. And at last I felt civilization encumber and oppress my consciousness, like cold fog brooding over a forest. I could not stand it any longer."

"But, Broad Shoulders, after you fled from the white man, you must have missed the customs and comforts that you had got used to."

"Ah, yes, for a while, as I said. But, for the most part, it was precisely the *customs* of civilization that I could not adjust to. Life became so preoccupied, so organized and instructed for observing the practices of civilization; there came to be a dichotomy between my original, uncultured nature and all the programs, rituals, liturgies. I felt a tired, impotent anger of the kind that seizes one who is attacked and cornered without reason and without avail. I thought: if it were now the custom, or the prevailing fashion, for people to walk on their hands—what a shriek of amazement would be heard if someone were to walk on his feet. That's how I looked upon cultured life. I thought the whole civilized world went around in black clothes."

"And you like it better in those you have on than in the black?"

"Yes, oh yes, I prefer my clothes as much as the white man prefers his. I only wish I could do without the vest and the trousers, but if I took them off I would freeze. It is the custom—"

"Yes, it's the custom. And now do you want to be an Indian all the rest of your life, Broad Shoulders?"

"Yes, now I want to be what I *am*. I now live the only way I can. And I am transported with joy and jubilation when I am on the trackless plains and in the Nature that I am a living part of. And I cleanse my spear in the mountain bear's breast and I eat the buffalo's broiled, still-smoking udder. And I lie down in the cool of the dew when night falls and the birds in the trees become silent, and I waken when the sentinel's yell warns of approaching danger. That's what I call 'real' life, because it is natural life."

Here Broad Shoulders put his hand on his chest and bent his elastic upper body forward. That was his farewell. Silently, limberly, he made his way out through the tepee's opening.

We sat back down. A moodiness came over me. I felt sorry for the proud young half-breed who was lost to organized life, to civilization, for which he was certainly well-endowed in many respects. But I could not help feeling a bit sad also about that life whose essential character he scorned so much—the life he had to give up because it was too "strictly laid out and taught" for him.

I looked around in the tepee. Fifteen members of the chief's entourage reclined or sat around the fire. Some of the women were making beadwork, others doing nothing, while the only three males, young teenagers, lay on their bellies and broiled buffalo meat on the coals. Nothing could be heard except the crackle of the burning twigs; no one spoke or paid any attention to anyone else. Apathetic and animal-like, they sat apart and brooded over their own, separate thoughts. There was not a trace of life in these dirty, meat-red faces with fixed, expressionless eyes; and the long, sharp-nailed, soiled hands grasped things mechanically. To get an old woman to look up from her knees, at which she had been staring for at least sixty minutes, I lay down and looked up in her face. She didn't move; her gaze remained fixed, grazing the side of my head. Then I gave up on her.

The tepee itself, which covered an area of about two hundred square feet, was made of thick canvas stretched over slender poles. Through an opening in the top, light entered and smoke escaped. But a lot of the smoke remained inside, along with an almost unbearable stench, as if from rotting carrion. Tobacco smoke smelled delightfully fresh in this heavy, dead air, as the chief and my friend calmly and quietly puffed away. Eventually Yellow Thunder bent toward the fire to scoop up a coal with his pipe.

Then I was able to glimpse, behind him, a young Indian maiden lying on her stomach and resting her head on her crossed arms. I was struck by the beauty of her form and by the strange position she had assumed. Involuntarily I moved to another deerskin so as to get a better look at her. She then sat up, pulled a wool blanket over her shoulders, and remained sitting with her upper body bare, while she stared apathetically down at her hands, which she clasped around her drawn-up knees. I could not help admiring this brown beauty with her filled-out shape and her indiscreet posture. Her lush, luxuriant hair was so black it seemed almost blue; her mouth remained closed, but the red of her lips was visible. She was beautiful. But her dead, emotionless gaze, which nothing could make attentive, gave her an unconscious expression, like that of a fatted animal. (I thought of a wounded buffalo I once saw lie down and stolidly bleed to death.) Her unconsciousness annoyed me, and when I had watched her for quite a while without making the slightest movement, I reached out and laid my hand on her bare shoulder. She slowly turned around and I was disconcerted to find she actually *could* look up. I asked her in English what her name was.

In back of me the chief said: "The 'tepee girl' does not understand the white man's language."

She sank back down into her previous position. At that, I was reminded of Darwin. How long should an Indian girl lie on her stomach and chew on her tongue before she becomes a perceptive and clarified being like the rest of us? And how long had girls lain that way since the time their ancestors hung in trees like monkeys? For the situation is not the same with the Indians' women as it is with their men; the latter are generations ahead of the former.

I remained silent and depressed at seeing, in a single day, so much beauty and vitality gone to waste: first the young, fiery half-breed and then this—this aimless creature. There was a rustle of the Indian girl's tall headfeather: she was lying down.

I now concentrated on listening to the chief, who had begun to talk to my friend again. To my great delight, he was explaining the tribe's religion, and since I did not want to miss any of what I thus was about to hear at first hand, I once more proceeded to take notes.

According to the tribe's teaching, one must renounce drunkenness and incest while living, and after death the Great Spirit would come and transport the still viable element to a new dwelling place. In its details this reli-

gion had similarities and points of contact with other religions; thus its doc-
trine of atonement and punishment was, in many respects, old and familiar from Christianity. There were those in the tribe who defied the Great
Spirit's will; they made their mothers and sisters pregnant, betrayed their
comrades on the warpath, and got drunk on firewater and wine.[2] So they
were punished after they died. Throughout seven times[3] they were denied
the Great Spirit's mercy. They could hear the noise of the hunt coming
from where the blessed were,[4] and they were excited by the cries of victory on the warpath. But all that was on the other side of a great mountain,
and while they could catch the joyful sounds they were not allowed over
there. Then, at the end of the seven times, there would come a judgment
from "the wide hunting grounds, wider than the earth." Scales would be
hung above the high mountain; in one pan would be blood, steaming animal blood, weighed out by the Great Spirit himself; in the other pan, the
sinner. If the blood should prove the heavier, he would have to atone for
seven more times, which would last only half as long as the first seven. But
if he outweighed the blood, he would hear over there, on the other side of
the mountain, much loud rejoicing over the hunt, and he would behold
great expanses where game ran far and wide, and he would sense a wild,
sweet, consuming desire for the plains fluttering through him and making
him feel faint. And in that brief explosive moment he would catch a
glimpse of tribes on the warpath over there, with plumes waving and billowing brightly in the sunlight, with tightly drawn bows on their shoulders
and gleaming steel-tipped arrows in their quivers. And when he heard the
chief's signal he would respond with yearning and the thirsty desire for jubilation—but then he would be reweighed and put back in his Hades. But
what he saw over there on the other side of the mountain would spur him
to live a purer life during the next atonement period, and then a roaring
spirit would carry him across when the short seven times were up. A per-

2. The Indians know the art of making wine out of palm juice and a kind of strong beer
out of corn and cassava root. They say that when they imbibe this special brew they are afraid
of nothing.

3. The chief explained, in response to a question, that this concept "seven times" was syn-
onymous with "seven periods," each of which was "longer than he could imagine."

4. Like other primitive peoples, the Indians have a material or physical conception of eternal life; for them, it is a place where swords clank merrily and one can chase wild game over
splendid hunting grounds.

son seldom needed more than two periods of seven times to "go over." Yellow Thunder knew only one whose sin the Great Spirit had punished more severely; that was a young warrior who assassinated his chief. He was doomed to wade through seven rivers every seventh day here on earth, besides the punishment he endured up there by "the mountain." Out of him came a sound like a mountain range baying at the moon; Yellow Thunder himself had seen and heard him twice. That is how he knew about it.

Many, however, attained the hunting grounds directly and without having to go through the seven times of trouble. These were the ones who brought to the scales the sacrificial blood that was weighed against the others.

I now asked whether they had sacred books such as other religions did.

"Oh, no," but I must not have the least doubt about the genuineness and truth of this religion. It had been handed down from one generation to another, from the moment countless "times" ago when the Great Spirit leveled the great hunting plains and let the rivers flow over dry courses. That is how old it was. And if I could decipher the red man's writing, I would learn that there were trees and rocks in holy places in Winnie Wony's [the Great Spirit's] forest that revealed mankind's age and the earth's first morning, and that described the great flood, in which the earth rolled about, a flood larger than could be imagined.

Were all Indians of the same faith?

"Oh, no," there were tribes without "times" or the "mountain" or the "great flood." One tribe worshiped a cowbell.

Here my friend broke out in laughter, forgetting what he himself had impressed upon me: not to laugh in Yellow Thunder's presence. The chief forgave him but could not be persuaded to say anything more about religion.

As the sun sank in the west, a soft breeze cooled the tepee. We took our leave of the friendly chief and his people. I approached the young beauty. "She is asleep," said Yellow Thunder, but she was not.

"Take care of yourself," I said and stroked her hair once. She lifted herself and looked at me. A kind of understanding surely moved through the tepid bog of her brain.

Outside, Broad Shoulders waved good-bye from the entrance of his tepee. It was like a last farewell—yes, like the last.

Mark Twain

Mark Twain's The Adventures of Huckleberry Finn *appeared the year before this essay was published in* Ny Illustreret Tidende *(Christiania) in three installments, March 22, 29, and April 5, 1885, but Hamsun had not had time to read that novel before leaving America. If he had read it, he would hardly have characterized Twain as lacking in fine irony. Twain was speaking in New York at the time Hamsun was in the city en route back to Norway, and Hamsun took advantage of the opportunity to hear him. Having tried his own skill at lecturing, Hamsun was particularly interested in Twain's platform technique.*

*I*n a country like America—where intellectual powers are devoted almost exclusively to material interests and are rapidly used up in the exhausting pursuit of social importance and influence—we should not expect to find the newest of the new or the highest development in either literature or art. Individual brilliance is constrained by social conditions. First of all, you must be an American *citizen* with the merit and respect which that implies; you can only be an individual afterward. Most of the surplus mental energy goes into projects for political and social well-being; little is left for the merely aesthetic.

To find evidence of this fact, you need only go to an exhibition of American paintings. You will find a slick daubing of strong colors, stiff figures on a blue or green background: a hand-painted *print* with a measured, mechanical technique and quite a bit of refined mixing of paint. The pictures are visual amusement. True, an American painter won a gold medal at the last Paris Exhibition. But this only goes to show that, among these 51 million Americans, one was finally found who could paint a picture with some content in it.

Or, to find evidence of the same thing, you can leaf through American literature, that literature of yesterday. It is not really authorship; it is fabrication, pretense, magazine literature, full of bad verse and common-school morality. Three names stand out above the magazine level, three authors who have taught themselves to write verse in the manner of Byron and Moore. They are Longfellow, Bryant, and Whitman. Longfellow, though, would probably not have been translated so widely and mentioned so often if he were not the poet who preeminently represents the lyric element in the world's greatest and richest country.

It is precisely because of the Americans' behavior, their lifestyle and social arrangements, that their writing has had such difficulty in maturing and achieving a breakthrough into more original forms. Hence their literature, even when viewed as one of the most "recent," does not show exceptional richness. Besides, it is utterly lacking in marks of national character; even the greatest writers have been unable to free themselves from the English models. The public spirit—which demands that the individual be first and foremost a *United States* citizen—is less particular with regard to literature, which does not need to be especially *national* to qualify as American. This explains why the American book market is still flooded with and dominated by the old English literary works, which are reprinted in Boston and New York in all possible editions and the greatest variety of formats.

Paradoxically, the same conditions that hamper a breakthrough of national literature also promote the development of a distinctively American kind of writing. In general, this kind of writing cannot properly be said to represent a people, but in America it has come, with its quantity and its peculiar character, to be a literary and cultural force, one that is more widespread and has far greater individuality than the rest of the literature. I refer to *humorous writing*. Absorbed as the American is with his material striving, and preoccupied as he is with his busy life on the gallop, he still has time to read his newspapers—and the humorists.

In the midst of this fermenting mass of people, the writing of amusing sketches has taken hold with steadily rising interest. Bryant, Emerson, Longfellow, and Poe stand in their places on a shelf, shining in their gilt bindings and decorating the room, but seldom taken down for a thorough reading. The humorists, however, are constantly being quoted and discussed; they live in the people in a way that almost no other element of the intellectual culture does. The reason is that the American as a rule has neither the time nor the patience to immerse himself in reading. The lingering, rather melancholy gentleness of Longfellow, the profound nature symbolism of Bryant, or the newness and unintelligibility of Whitman—he soon gets bored with these and either dozes off or is provoked to impatience. But the humorists, with their short, easy-to-read pieces, can be enjoyed without effort during the noon pause or in the evening when the day's struggle is over. Besides, the American in general is more inclined to the comic, to noisy fun, than to introspective meditations. Profundities, thoughtful and penetrating views, are not his thing. In his aesthetic pleasures, too, there must be garish colors for his eyes and trip-hammer blows for his ears. And these are what the humorists provide.

America has a total of six humorists. Here in Norway we are well acquainted with only two: Mark Twain and Bret Harte. The other four are Irving, Holmes, Lowell, and Artemus Ward.

While Bryant is undoubtedly America's greatest lyric genius, though much less read than Longfellow and almost never translated, Irving is the foremost, the finest, the most intelligent humorist the country has ever had. But he was influenced by new currents during his travels in Europe, especially by the French *esprit,* and he became a bit too subtle for his fellow countrymen, so that he now is almost forgotten in comparison with the noisier humorists who have recently appeared. Both Holmes and Lowell write in a lengthy, solid style; they aim mostly to make an impression by means of quantity, and they frequently use gloomy images. Holmes, by the way, is more inclined to be critical and has written some monographs that are still cited. Artemus Ward, that sharp, dazzling, witty gentleman, has *talked* more than he has written (like him, Mark Twain has held public lectures and has taken the intelligent public by storm).

These four deserve the title of humorist about as much as Bret Harte, who is just as properly known as a poet, and he most often treats his material more as a poet than as a humorist. There is more to being a humorist than the ability to use grotesque, colossal exaggerations, and it is something quite other than the ability to write moving, touching depictions of life in the mining towns. What, on the one hand, are qualifications become hindrances on the other hand. We shall dwell a little longer on Mark Twain, the greatest and most popular representative of American humor writing.

Samuel Langhorne Clemens, alias Mark Twain, was born in Florida, deep down in the American South [actually, in the town of Florida, Missouri], in 1835. This brilliant funmaker, who has now had a European reputation for more than fifteen years, is thus a man of fifty. As a small boy he worked in a newspaper composing room, then supported himself as a book printer, and, when a little older, became a river pilot, mainly on the Mississippi. You can hardly read a line of Twain without noticing the typographical influence on it. His punctuation, even for American English, is so abundant it seems it would use up all the commas and periods of a printery well supplied with them. He got his pen name from his life as a riverboat pilot. Time and again he heard the call "Mark Twain," or "two fathoms," and when he began to work on newspapers he wrote his name *Mark Twain.* In 1861 he went to Nevada, where he served as private secretary to his brother, the territorial secretary, in that wild and lonely silver-mining country. In *Roughing It* Twain later gave a description of life there. The book presents what he himself did and what he did not do but others did— a sketch of great originality and tremendous verbal force. In 1864 [1866] he was in the Hawaiian Islands, and from there he has brought such a description of boiling craters, white-glowing crystals, and lava pouring out over mile-long stretches that the poor devils who only have been to Vesuvius had best be quiet about their ridiculously trivial experiences. Twain debuted as a humorous writer in 1867 with *The Jumping Frog and Other Sketches,* most of which are better than *Frog* but none of them better known. In 1869 he married a rich woman out there in the West [he married Olivia Langdon in Elmira, New York, in 1870] but was soon on his travels again, this time to Europe and the Holy Land [this trip was made in 1867]. In 1872 he made a lecture tour of England. Meanwhile, besides being a river pilot and a secretary, he was a gold digger, editor, and land speculator.

Travel is Twain's real source of inspiration; he likes to roam around and make notes along the way. That is why his style is so lively, unpredictable, and startling, his images often so far-fetched, so far-out. In the midst of a depiction of Western journalism, where newspapers are edited as much with a revolver as with a pen, he suddenly remembers some idyllic little event from Syria and proceeds to rivet it into the same piece. Or when describing a solemn moment in front of marble Greek gods, he can use expressions gathered from the colloquial speech of the wild Sierra. But this impairs the sense less often than it does the aesthetic pleasure. Most often it gives the reader the surest impression of what the author has tried to illustrate, for the images generally are strikingly original and unexpected. These are images that never miss the mark with Americans. Take the man who had drunk so much soda pop and swelled up so much that the only item in his wardrobe he could use that day was his umbrella, or the man who was so tall he had to get down on his knees when he wanted to stick his hand in his pants pocket, or the man who was so short he had to stand on a chair when he wanted to put on his hat, or the trees that were so tall it took two men to look at them, since one alone could see no higher than halfway up the trunk—this is his kind of absurdly exaggerated but by no means senseless Yankee humor. His bold and natural truthfulness, his openness, helps considerably to make him clear to the reader. He has made direct, minute observations and has accumulated such a wealth of them from his travels that you seldom if ever get from his books the impression of artificial or invented analogies.

The fact that Twain has been out and gained personal experience places him in a position not only to be artistically secure but also to be *fair* in his judgments, if only in his own way, that is, from the standpoint of a man exceedingly ill equipped with formal learning. True, Twain can overlook or make fun of things that deserve to be treated otherwise, but where he aims to be factual (as, for example, in *The Innocents Abroad*), he is fair—in his own way—fair to the wild miner without going into panegyrics the way Bret Harte does, fair regarding the travelers' eccentricities whether he finds them among the Englishmen or the Germans, the Frenchmen or the Americans, and always fair in regard to religion. Never does he laugh at it or show disrespect, though his remarks are sometimes a bit freer than many people like to see sacred things treated. In his case, however, this is more a lack of taste than a lack of religious feeling; he is himself a Christian and, as such, comes closest to being a Presbyterian.

Twain's kind of humor is open, easily intelligible clown-caricature, market-stall comedy, which everybody can understand. Twain is no introspective man, no fine ironist who stands there with a supercilious smile and makes cutting remarks; he comes out roaring with laughter—and strikes. His banter, though light, has a rough power. It amuses as soon as it is comprehended, and it is comprehended as soon as it is read. You do not need to look behind the words to find the laughter-provoking element—which is an advantage, since slow comprehension always lessens the effect of a joke. Artemus Ward gathers all his elegant wit into a single sentence and uses a half or a whole page to prepare for the next sentence of the same kind. Twain does not do this. He spreads out his fun, lets his witticisms fall drop by drop, and thereby, besides arousing amusement and laughter, creates a *poetic image*, which it would be less urgent or perhaps even impossible for Ward to form. Twain's gift is an intense though spun-out humor, carefully planned so that at times, whenever necessary, it becomes an American *flash*, a concentrated shower of wit and jest. While Irving, who constantly tries to strike someone or something with his brilliant polemic, always holds himself back for fear of possible attacks, Twain always walks nonchalantly as if with revolvers in his belt and bowie knives in his boot tops—always without second thoughts and always without regard to the prevailing rules.

Some have attempted to make Twain into a great, daring satirist constantly carrying on with his ridicule against corruption in American society, but nobody can fall into this error except those who are unacquainted with the conditions under which a man in America must write. True, Twain is one of those humorists who tell truthful lies, and what he says is true in its way, thanks to his sense of reality and his thorough studies of nature. But it leads far from an "understanding" of him when anyone looks for polemic in all his boisterousness. There is already evidence of this forced inventiveness in articles about him. I would not like to be in Twain's place if he thought of reforming, of "wanting" something, when he wrote the two stories, one about the bad little boy and the other about the good little boy. I say, God have mercy on him if he meant what he said about the republic's great hero Washington!

Twain is by no means a European author, interested in finding veiled meanings, hidden thoughts. He is simply a straightforward, fun-loving American who no doubt can mock and scoff but who knows the people he is writing for, and most of them only want to be amused. What most often misleads people into a determined effort to find meaning behind Twain's words is the minute description he uses in his sketches, description that is full of natural truth, omitting nothing, whether or not it fits in with what he is writing about. This kind of description seems unnecessary to the non-American reader, unless the author wants thereby to let the reader understand what "lies at the bottom." With Twain, who has observations in stock and never uses allegory, this is just his way of writing and nothing else.

I do not mean to say that Twain never polemicizes, but only that I have seldom had the honor to be informed about it by the author himself. He does it once in anger and lets his meaning, though ostensibly hidden, shine through the paradox. This is especially the case in his *The Innocents Abroad* and *The New Pilgrim's Progress* [the separately published parts one and two of the book Americans know as *The Innocents Abroad*], records and recollections of his great travels in Europe and the Orient. These books, which he himself and many others consider his major works, contain quite a few open confessions and bold judgments, thus giving an excellent insight into the author's inner self. He exposes his narrow-mindedness and his undeveloped philosophy of life, while he also shows himself to be, by virtue of his nationality, a genuine Son of Freedom, a democrat, in contradistinction to the unfree and downtrodden people he meets on his travels.

At the beginning of June 1867 the steamship *Quaker City* started from New York Harbor on a pleasure trip, went through the Mediterranean Sea and along the coasts of Spain, France, Italy, Turkey, Greece, Egypt, and Syria, and was back in New York by autumn. Twain went along, together with three preachers, eight doctors, sixteen women, and several military and naval officers. His fame had grown by that time. He was living in San Francisco as editor of the Nevada *Territorial Enterprise* and was ranked as one of the masters of the new California literature. Without much forethought or advance planning, he embarked solely to gain background information, to tour the world and see things as they actually were, and thus to enrich his already multifarious personal experiences.

From this tour came the two thick volumes *The Innocents Abroad* and *The New Pilgrim's Progress*. Both of them mixed anger with humor and bared other people's shortcomings as well as the author's own, especially his poor qualification for rightly judging the conditions and the human beings of Europe. He came from a remote part of a country itself remote, from his beloved miners, those uneducated, hardfisted bandits, among whom it was a mark of merit for one to have "killed his man." Now he was sailing out into the world to look at European life and art! How did he react to the new and great things he got to see? Quite consistently—as a humorist and an ignoramus.

Instinctively, in accordance with his usual practice, he was poised to make fun of everything that was foreign to him as a democrat. In his superpatriotic self-centeredness he was hurt and embittered by everything that differed from the customs of his native land, and he was utterly incapable of appreciating the art. He himself relates that it was one of his greatest pleasures to drive his hosts to despair on account of his indifference and stupidity—a behavior that is not only naive self-delusion but also characteristic of all barbarians who want to amount to something.

Thus he has more real feeling for the amazing industrial development of his home country than for the art of Europe, and a greater appreciation of the California settlers' houses than of Europe's historic ruins. He has an eye for what strikes him as practical, speculative life. Railroad stations, big ship lines, boulevards, banks, wholesale warehouses—these things interest him much more than do all the art galleries put together. He understands the former but lacks the education, experience, and perspective to judge the latter. At Notre Dame Cathedral he notices practically nothing but the relics, which he views as ridiculous. The masterworks of the Louvre become for the democrat merely a pretext for him to declaim against the base adulation on the part of the artists, who have prostituted their talent by placing the ruling tyrants on the clouds as gods. He bestows greater attention on the Julian Column than it deserves, only to get an occasion to curse the site of the Bastille. At the Chateau d'If he views the prison of Monte Cristo with the same interest as that of the Man in the Iron Mask, and he confuses Catherine with Maria de Medici and Raphael with Rubens. He envies connoisseurs for their admiration of paintings which in his opinion are quite incomprehensible—such as, for example, Leonardo da Vinci's *The Last Supper*. He envies them for their ability to *enjoy* looking at art, just as he envies all Europeans who are ahead of the Americans.

This kind of patriotism, which Twain shares with all his fellow Americans, might possibly be excused if it were not, in his case, mixed with an almost boyish personal vanity. The same Twain who imposes the harshest judgments on the poor Turks finds little or nothing wrong with Russia, that European absolutism, where material could nevertheless be found for a Twain-democratic joke about folios. Why is he so gentle? Well, the czar has given the wild man from the West an audience! and the czarina and Princess Marie have spoken English with him! Later he and his fellow travelers are taken around the Yalta palace by Alexander himself; are invited to visit Crown Prince Michael; have breakfast with dukes, princes, admirals, and honorable ladies; and must receive Prince Dulgorouki himself and Baron Wrangel himself! And during all this, Twain clearly becomes preoccupied with the idea of showing courtesies. The emperors and aristocrats no longer seem so detestable; Mark Twain has fallen out with the democrat!

It goes otherwise with him in Italy, where his self-centered patriotism collides with the inhabitants' ignorance of things in his homeland, exactly the same kind of ignorance that foreigners suffer from when they go to America. With an indignation that verges on anger, Twain here is compelled to admit that all the churches in all the American cities together cannot buy so many art treasures as are owned by a single one of Italy's hundreds of cathedrals. But he consoles himself with wondering why—and actually losing himself in reverie over it—nobody has yet been smart enough to propose that these artworks be thrown into the bankrupt public treasury, where they would be assets worth millions. He despises and detests Italy; as a practical American, he sees it on the verge of bankruptcy, and he simply cannot comprehend why this poverty-stricken country will put up with the scandal of the swollen magnificence that is laid on the graves of the Medici.

The same kind of national pride shows up in his attitude toward Pompeii. This place annoys him to the point of wrath because there is still enough of it left that we can study its history and its residences in the smallest detail. If lava should bury an American city, we would hardly find a single ruin of any significance under the ashes! Regarding the architectural superiority of Paris over the towns in the Sierra Nevada, Twain consoles himself a bit with the quip that the hotels have no soap and the streets no gas in Paris. With that, and with the Parisian chambermaids' negligence when they make up his room, he jumps to the conclusion that the French lack any sense of tidiness or punctuality.

He has seen Napoleon III and Napoleon's guest the sultan. For Twain these two represent, reasonably enough, full-blown despotism, ignorance, and superstition. But the first of the two has what "neither the fiasco in Strasbourg nor the imprisonment in Ham has been able to deprive him of:

the genius of energy, endurance, and the spirit of enterprise." He it is who sent his cry of "Forward!" out over Europe, who rebuilt Paris, who rebuilt nearly all the cities in his country and put them so far ahead of the rustic towns in Nevada! This little man—with the handlebar mustache, the withered, impenetrable face, and the cunning eyes—possesses a *self-reliance*, a *craft*, and an *endurance* that make him a great speculator, a thoroughgoing adventurer, an *American fellow!* Mark Twain's own words! Napoleon III *could* have been an American!

The Orient does not please Twain; its idling, dreaming poetry is too inactive, too immobile for that positive man. He almost wishes that Turkey were fated to collapse, and he would not mind if it were laid waste by his friend the czar. Even in Palestine, though he feels more at home there, he cannot reconcile himself with the conditions he finds. His primitive vigor is opposed to the unprogressive, unproductive, worship-driven way of life.

You get the feeling that, on the entire journey, he is under the influence of his frontier nature, which will not give him elbowroom, will not allow the humorist to appear in his unreflecting individuality. There must be more iconoclasm; there must be a show of good American democratic will. Thus, in the eyes of a European, the books about "the pleasure trip on the Continent" are far inferior to the same man's writings on his less noticed and less extensive excursions in his own country. Not that they are spiritless or less entertaining; they are full of humor and spirit, witty thoughts, and clever paradoxes; here the beauties of nature also find an intelligent observer in Twain. But these books are marred by their bad polemic, absurdly underdeveloped philosophy, and weak powers of reflection. You are not thus embarrassed by Twain's accounts of his trips in his homeland, where he knows his way about and just lets the humor rustle softly through the leaves.

Twain is no statesman, and he is a politician only to the extent that every other American citizen is. To go to Europe and be a critic requires other qualifications than his energy and generally sound instincts. He is to be fully trusted only when he is dealing with the mining regions, where rich ores lie underfoot, where men shoot each other for sport, and where they fight their way through the impartial air, between outlaws and Indians, over ice fields and deserts. Here he is at home, and no other American has as yet surpassed him in telling what is queer or funny: his powers of invention, boundless imagination, and original style are precisely the qualities that are needed here. They are less useful when it comes to studies of Greek antiques or European theories of government.

There is a similarity between Twain's works and his physical person. About him there is little of the fine or delicate. He has the movements of a miner, is quite lacking in taste and tact, and constantly sets himself above the generally accepted rules. As a public lecturer, he has none of the lyric gestures with which Ingersoll illustrates his ideas, and none of the supple grace with which the fine Artemus Ward appears before his audience. Twain's gestures on the platform are more like the sign language that accompanies a "Psst!" to the waiter, or the motion a person makes when getting ready to pick up an armful of hay. When he warms up in the course of the speech, the little man becomes excited and clenches his thin hands with a sort of lustiness, as if his audience were a desperate bunch of mineworkers to whom it was necessary to show his fist. As a rule he talks slowly, very slowly indeed, and seldom looks at any individual among his listeners. The listeners do not laugh loud or long; with Twain, there are no bolts of lightning, no takings by storm; nobody falls into uncontrollable laughter, like that which used to interrupt Artemus Ward during his lecture and leave him so comically amazed. Twain's speeches are entertaining but have absolutely no content. You sit there in suspense, waiting for the introduction to end and the lecture to begin, until Twain suddenly makes his bow—and leaves. It's all over! You look at the clock: an hour and twenty minutes. What can this mean? It means, my dear, that Mark Twain is a genuine public lecturer. If he says anything, he says it well. But in the art of talking for more than an hour and saying next to *nothing,* yet keeping his audience interested—in that art he can give the best parliamentary speakers a run for their money.

"Maybe you think it's now time for me to begin. A cynic said to me one day: 'Do you know what makes a good speaker?' 'I haven't the slightest idea,' I answered. 'Well, the first thing is knowing what to leave out.' 'That's good,' I thought. 'The next thing is knowing what to put in.' 'That's even better.' 'And do you know what the last thing is?' he asked. 'I give up.' 'That's knowing when to stop.' 'The best of all,' I said. My friend grimly looked me over: 'And do you know which of these three things I advise most people to begin with?' 'No. Which one?' I anxiously inquired. 'The last one.'

'Hm! Well,' I said, 'that doesn't give me much encouragement, but I will take the first three points into account.'"

That is a sample of Mark Twain's lecture. That is the way he stands and chats and quips. Even in his wildest sketches of Western mine life—with its orgies of gold, blood, and whiskey—there is a nice good-naturedness about him, a half-smile on his lips. In England his listeners did not understand him, and he went back home before they had time to get used to his unique kind of speechmaking. In America, however, where people can calmly and comfortably be told about robberies and scalpings, Twain has made a lot of money as a speaker. Time and again he has sparked the big cities of the East to laughter and joy. Americans are more familiar with his peculiar language, containing so much untranslatable slang. English is his basic tongue, but for the things he has to say, it is often too worn, too tired, and too small—capable of expressing no more than the old English civilization. New words are needed to represent new inventions, new ideas, new ways of life. Twain's language is therefore a mixture of the most diverse localisms and neologisms—powerful, sinewy, audacious expressions—like new shoots on the old linguistic stems. He has taken up, studied, and made use of American folk language, which blends everyday speech with Indian terms (civilized by the Anglo-Saxons) and with immigrant dialects. So it is the *people* who particularly understand and enjoy him.

A Bonanza Farm

Oliver Dalrymple was manager and half-owner of a wheat farm near Cassel-
ton, Dakota Territory, that covered more than 115 square miles. In 1880, when
only a third of its land was under cultivation, the farm employed 600 men, 115
self-binding reapers, and 71 steam threshers. Hamsun described working condi-
tions on the Dalrymple farm in a letter dated "Dakota, September 1887," which
he sent to Verdens Gang *(Christiania), and which that newspaper published on*
November 10, 1887.

The Great Plains of Dakota Territory are gradually being occupied. Everything here is on a grand scale. The land itself reminds you of the ocean—
green, billowing, vast distances without a tree, with only a house here and
there that appears to swim in the sea of grass. Here the tracts are not measured in acres but usually in miles, square miles, a farm being said to be so
many miles large. To cultivate these expanses, you need a multitude of men
and the operation of the American kind of huge machinery. Plows, drawn
not by horses but by tractors, turn as many as twenty-two furrows at a time.
Throughout the autumn, steam-powered threshing machines whir and
roar all day long. During the summer a big Red River Valley farm swarms
with people, like a small city. Oliver Dalrymple, for instance, employs a
work force of twelve to fourteen hundred men.

Oliver Dalrymple came here fifteen years ago and appropriated a tract
of a hundred thousand acres of wheat land, measuring five and a half Norwegian miles [about forty American miles] on each side. To run this monstrous estate, he has a manager over each division, and he has foremen, office people, his own store, blacksmith shop, painters, carpenters, wagon
makers, etc. He has a small, steam-powered mill that produces only his own

flour. He harvests 1.5 million bushels of wheat a year. The nearest railroad station bears Dalrymple's name.

I have spent a summer at this man's place. You might say he knows how to run a farm, but none of his workers like him. Bad food, a fourteen-to-fifteen-hour workday, and low wages. Add to all that the rich man's arbitrary use of his authority.

The workers are drummed out for breakfast at three or half past three in the morning, so early that it is still completely dark. The foremen, astride their horses, are already waiting, and the wagons are rolling forth to take the labor force out to the fields. It is still early, and the ground is white with thick, cold frost, for the nights are so chilly here in the West.

In an hour or two the sun will rise, pouring out light, and the earth will smoke with mist. The heat will increase until two or three o'clock in the afternoon, when it is at its highest. It is often unbearable, the sun beating down on your head, and no shade to be found anywhere. The ground gets so hot it burns through your shoe soles and makes your feet sore. The laborers wear light, thin shirts that do not absorb too much sun. One day during the haying when a mule collapsed from sunstroke, we left it lying and took another one in its place. Watching from his saddle, the foreman ordered us to get under the hay wagons. We lay there for two hours, until the worst of the heat was over. There was a little tear in my shirt, at the shoulder, where I felt a soreness. The skin was broken, leaving an open sore, and my whole shoulder was swollen. At first I thought I had been bitten by some insect or other, but I was merely burned by the sun.

After the midday meal—a miserable lunch of spoiled meat and beans, which we eat out in the field—we get a little rest, up to an hour when cutting hay, only a few minutes when harvesting and threshing wheat. We crawl under the wagons and try to nap. But we are constantly disturbed by the flies and all kinds of tiny creatures that swarm out from the grass. You people in Norway cannot imagine what a frightful variety there is around here of tiny creeping, flying, and jumping animals—strange, disgusting creatures—that sit and stare at us until we step on them and crush them. When harvesting and threshing, we are pestered by a little black bug that eats our clothes. The jacket with many round holes which the farmer wears when he visits the nearest prairie town shows the marks of this vermin's appetite.

How eagerly the worker looks forward to the night! After the terrible sun has finally set, he still has an hour or more of work left. Not until it begins to get dark does the foreman give the signal from his saddle, and each man throws down his pitchfork, exhausted, exploited to the uttermost. The eight-hour movement, so strong down East, has not yet reached us here in the West. Oliver Dalrymple uses his people for fourteen to fifteen hours of daily work and allows them only five or six hours of sleep.

It is a hard life for both man and beast out here. So, to get workers in harvest time, the large-scale farmers of the Red River Valley look mainly to Scandinavians, who can wear themselves out and keep quiet about it. I wish to emphasize this, so as to warn newcomers, for it is especially they who come out here.

Besides the bad food and long hours, there is another drawback, a dangerous one, and that is the *drinking water*, which all over Dakota is more or less noxious, containing as it does more alkali than anywhere else in America. When the summer heat was at its height, during the last days of July, almost all of Dalrymple's people got sick from the alkali water; only those with cast-iron stomachs were able to withstand its effects.

The nights are cold and quiet, with only the ceaseless sound of the grasshoppers to be heard out over the prairie. It is very dark, and the dew falls like fine rain. There are no birds here, except for the prairie chicken and now and then a solitary hawk that fearlessly and lazily sails right over our hats.

The ugliest sight in Dakota is the treatment of the poor mules, with deep sores under their shoulder pads. The most beautiful sight is the splendid sunset, the grandest in the world when the horizon foams in gold and blood.

Robert Ingersoll

Robert G. Ingersoll (1833–1899), though a highly successful lawyer and a prominent Republican politician, was best known to Americans as a freethinker and an orator. To Norwegians also he was best known for his antireligious views, some of which Bjørnstjerne Bjørnson translated. In listening to Ingersoll, Hamsun was more interested in the technique than in the content of his lectures. He wrote this account while living in Copenhagen after his second return from America, and the local periodical Politiken *published it on September 30, 1888.*

A private letter reports that Robert Ingersoll is extremely ill; in any case, his increasing corpulence will lead him day by day to death by apoplexy. Should he pass away now, the Republicans will lose a prop and America a god.

Right now his party needs all the active servants it possesses, not to defeat the Democrats in 1889 [1888]—that is a lost cause—but to combat the much more dangerous Prohibitionist party in the election of 1893 [1892]. These fanatics can already count on more than two million votes, and to judge by their fierce proselytizing, it is quite evident that they will elect their own president five years from now. The great Republican party is declining. For twenty-five years it ruled America, and Grover Cleveland's election four years ago was the first break in its power. Yes, it is declining. Grant is dead, Blaine old, Sheridan ill, and now its great advocate is collapsing. He has grown weak and is suffering.

There is no man in America whose name is better known than Ingersoll's, not any president's, not Henry George's. It has become a household word. When attorney Ingersoll takes a case, it is almost as good as won. And when he leaves his home in the East to speak in unfamiliar cities, his fans flock after him to listen again and again to the superb, impassioned preacher of humane morality. An impressive personality like Bjørnson, he has the same emotional electricity.

Ingersoll has made himself famous through his skill as a speaker. Not only does he possess a brute oratorical power, but he knows all the tricks of the trade and makes good use of them. Trained as a trial lawyer, he has been called to serve as a tribune. It had been hoped that he would take charge of the Chicago anarchists' case in 1886, and if he had done so, there is good ground for thinking the verdict would have been different. Even as an attorney, he is more a popular speaker than a legal expert, and he would have had an opportunity to display the qualities that have created his fame as a trial lawyer—his humane way of thinking and his intense pathos.

I have heard him talk about *Hell*. He was right in his element. The subject gave him an occasion to use his most crafty devices, his grossest effects, without which his half-educated public would have been bored. In front of the footlights, with a sea of humanity before his eyes, in the silence that comes with tense anticipation, he first feels his way ahead with some introductory remarks, gives out a little good-natured witticism, a bit of jargon, then grimaces and shrugs his broad shoulders so as to provoke laughter and lighten the mood. Having done that, he suddenly becomes serious and switches to pathos. He appeals to parental love ("Mother, think of a God who would send your child to hell because you had cursed a minister!"). He shows his political colors ("I would not even shove a Democrat down there"). And he speaks again and again to the audience's patriotic feelings ("Having got this glorious land to live in, I will live here to the end. I do not ask for any better paradise; I give up all claim to burning hereafter. What do you think? Would you rather go to hell? I will give you two minutes to think it over!"). And his public, who sit there quietly waiting for the next quip, listen wide-awake to every variation of this resounding ungodliness. But when the next witticism comes, the old farmers from the prairie howl, and the Republican officeholders from the city clap, stomp, and poke their canes and umbrellas on the floor, making a noise that can be heard over the entire block.

If a stranger passing by on the street asks what is going on inside, he will get a smile and the answer: "Don't you know that Ingersoll is in town?"

Ingersoll knows his people and he knows them well. As a political agitator he is excellent. The opinions he puts forth are generally those of the entire nation; his views are essentially the good old doctrines that amount to common wisdom. He is a child of his own people, this industrious, in many ways culturally unmodern people, for whom love of country is the most sacred feeling and the Unitarian Emerson the highest philosopher. When Ingersoll knows that his audience is mixed, he shows his great expertise by pitching his lecture at so precisely an average level as to keep everybody with him. There is no farmer whose head he goes over, no political opponent that he fails to provoke to laughter with his jokes. So it is taken for granted that Ingersoll is one of the Republican party's strongest supporters, that bringing him to a convention is like hauling in the last and heaviest artillery on the field. In his mouth the words become dramatic, take on strong colors, acquire a certain movement that everyone understands, and roll out so loudly as to keep people awake and rattle the windows in the hall. At the last convention in Chicago, however, he did not succeed in winning any victory. Not only was he indisposed and nervous, but he was standing in front of old, experienced politicians who were not so easy to turn around.

Reading Ingersoll's speeches is not the same as listening to them. For the most part, his writing is less effective than his oral presentation. His writings lack the piquant slang and the many bold tricks that occur to him during his lectures; what are left are some quite ordinary observations along with more or less skillful argumentation. In the most recent issues of the *North American Review* he carries on a theological discussion with Gladstone, in which he confronts the old statesman's knowledge with the familiar things from his lectures, with patriotism, morality, and common sense. More than once, to win an argument with his own country's clergymen and religious newspapers, he has resorted to drumming people together and delivering an oral reply.

No matter how Ingersoll behaves—makes mistakes, does crazy things—he remains his party's prop and his people's god. The reason for this is primarily that he has become an object of popular enthusiasm because of his eloquence, and secondarily that he has an elevated social standing. He is a colonel from the war, this war that so many Americans look upon as the only significant war in world history. He is a lawyer and, as such, enjoys boundless prestige. Finally, he is a rich man, a large property owner, which by itself is enough to make him a politician in his country—two-thirds of the members of the American Congress are millionaires.

Ingersoll can be as much of a freethinker as he wants to, can lose a political battle at a convention or a theological one during a dispute about Moses, but will never lose the enthusiasm of the Americans. The worst thing he can do to his people is to go off now and die. For where can they get another "Bob." With the naive hero worship that is characteristic of his countrymen, they keep an eye on the great man's every movement, telegraph his pronouncements, and attribute political and patriotic significance to even the smallest trip he takes. And the newspapers report his comings and goings as if he were a prince.

I once traveled with Ingersoll on a railroad train. In our coach there was a woman who simply could not get her screaming child to shut up. Ingersoll looked at her a while and then, out of sympathy, good-hearted as he is, took the child from her and finally lulled it to sleep. When the train arrived in Chicago and I got my hands on a newspaper, I read about this very event in an extra edition of the *Herald.*

MEMORY AND FANTASY
(1897–1905)

Terror

This story, first published in 1897, is based on an event that occurred thirteen years earlier, but Hamsun is either exercising poetic license or suffering from a memory lapse when he says Jesse James was captured and killed at Madelia. Jesse and his brother Frank escaped after their foiled bank robbery attempt in Northfield, Minnesota, in 1876. The three Younger brothers, who had joined in the Northfield raid, were captured near Madelia. Jesse James, however, enjoyed a notoriety that the Youngers could not match, and Hamsun might have thought that Madelia would acquire an aura of evil appropriate for his story if James were associated with the town.

I never really knew what fear was until that time during my first stay in America. Not that my courage was so great, but it had never been put to such a thorough test before. This was in the year 1884.

Out on the prairie lies a little town known as Madelia, a very depressing and unattractive place with its ugly houses, rough plank sidewalks, and ungracious people. This is where Jesse James, America's most bloodthirsty and trigger-happy bandit, was finally captured and killed. He had gone there to hide out—a fitting place for that monster who for many years had made the free states hazardous with his attacks, his plundering, and his murders.

I went there, too, but with a more peaceful aim, which was simply to help an acquaintance out of a difficulty. An American by the name of Johnston was a schoolteacher in a Wisconsin town, where I had got to know him and his wife. Some time later this man left schoolteaching for a more practical occupation: he moved to that prairie town of Madelia and went into the lumber business. After he had been in it for a year, I received a letter from him asking whether I could come to Madelia and run the business while he and his wife took a trip to the East. Being unemployed at the moment, I left for Madelia.

I arrived at the Madelia railroad station on a dark winter evening, was met by Johnston, went home with him, and was shown to my room. His house was located some distance outside of town. We spent much of the night with his explaining the fine points of the lumber business, all of it unfamiliar to me. The next morning Johnston jokingly handed me his revolver, and a couple of hours later he and his wife were on the train.

Now that I was alone in the house, I moved from my room to the living room, where I could make myself more comfortable and where, besides, I could better keep an eye on the whole house. I also began to use the Johnstons' bed.

The same routine went on for several days. I sold planks and boards and, every afternoon, took the day's cash accumulation down to the bank, where it was receipted in my bankbook.

There was nobody else in the house; I was all by myself. I got my own meals, milked and took care of Johnston's two cows, baked bread, boiled and broiled one thing and another. My first attempt at baking did not turn out very well; I used too much flour and did not bake the dough long enough, so the bread had raw streaks in it, and the next day it was hard as a rock. I was also unlucky the first time I tried to cook cereal. In the pantry I found a peck of nice pearl barley, which seemed ideal for cooking. I poured milk into a large casserole, then added barley and began to stir. I soon realized my mixture was too thick, so I added more milk. Then I stirred some more. But, as the stuff bubbled and boiled, the barley pearls swelled up as big as peas, and there was a shortage of milk again. The stuff was expanding so fast that the casserole was about to boil over. I began to ladle it out into cups and other containers, but it threatened to boil over anyhow. I found more cups and containers, and they all filled up. The casserole kept on wanting to boil over, and it kept on demanding milk—until the soup became as thick as pudding. Finally I had no other recourse, so I poured the entire contents of the casserole out on a board, just a plain old board. The contents flowed over it like lava, to make a lovely mess, lying quite still, good and thick, hardening as it lay there.

Now I had *materia prima,* so to speak, and whenever I wanted cereal after that, I merely cut off a piece of the stuff on the board, mixed milk with it, and boiled it again. I ate it heroically for all my meals, every day, to get rid of it. To tell the truth, this was hard work, but I knew absolutely no one in the town I could invite to help me. And finally I finished the job alone.

For a man of twenty-some years, all by himself, it was quite lonely in that big house. The nights were cold and dark, and there was no neighbor in any direction until you got to town. Still, I was not afraid and had no reason to be. And when, two evenings in a row, I thought I heard a suspicious noise, like someone fooling with the lock on the kitchen door, I got up, took a lamp with me, and checked the door both inside and outside. But I found nothing wrong with the lock. And I did not pick up the revolver.

A night was to come, though, when I would be seized by a terror more hair-raising than anything I ever experienced before or since. And for a long time afterward I suffered from that night's experience.

That day I was unusually busy, closing several big transactions and being tied up with work all afternoon. By the time I finally finished, it was so late that it was quite dark and the bank was closed. Since I could not deposit the day's cash, I took it home with me and counted it in the living room: it came to $700 or $800.

That evening, as usual, I sat down to do some writing. It grew later and later as I sat and wrote. Midnight came, and then two o'clock. Suddenly I again heard that mysterious fiddling with the kitchen door. What was it?

There were two outer doors to the house: the one that led into the kitchen and another, the main entrance, that led into a hallway in front of the living room. For security, I had propped this front door shut with a beam on the inside. The living room had window shades of a patented kind, so tight that from the outside a person could see absolutely no light from the lamp.

And now there was that noise at the kitchen door.

I picked up the lamp, went and stood near the door, and listened. Someone was out there; I could hear whispering and the squeaking of footsteps in the snow. I listened for quite a while. The whispering stopped, and the squeaking steps seemed to move farther away. Then all became quiet.

I went back to the living room and sat down to write again. A half hour went by.

Suddenly I was so startled I felt as if I jumped out of my skin. The front door was being smashed in. Not only the lock but the prop inside the door snapped, and I heard steps in the hallway right outside the inner door of the living room. The break-in was possible only with a hard running start and with the combined efforts of more than one person, for the prop was quite strong.

My heart did not beat—it quivered. I made no outcry, not a sound, but I felt the agitation of my heart all the way up in my throat, and it kept me from breathing properly. For a few seconds I was so terrified I hardly knew where I was. Then it occurred to me that I must save the money, so I went into the bedroom, took my wallet out of my pocket, and stuck it under the bedclothes. After that, I went back to the living room, the whole operation having surely taken less than a minute.

There was muffled talking outside the door, along with the sound of its lock being picked. I took out Johnston's revolver and examined it. It worked. My hands shook violently, and my legs could hardly hold me up.

My eyes fell upon the door. It was unusually solid, made of planks with heavy crosspieces. It was, you might say, not carpentered but timbered together. Encouraged by the massiveness of the door, I again began to think—which up to now I certainly had not been doing. The door opened outward and consequently could not be broken in, especially since the hallway out there was too short to allow a running start. As I realized this, I suddenly became quite a plucky fellow. I yelled that anyone coming in would die on the spot. Nobody but me could have understood what I was saying, since I was speaking Norwegian. Realizing the stupidity of this, I repeated my threat loudly in English. No answer. To get my eyes used to the darkness in case the windows should be broken in and the lamp go out, I immediately put out the light. I now stood in the dark, with my eyes directed toward the windows and with the revolver in my hand. Time dragged on. Growing bolder and bolder, I dared to act like a hell of a fellow.

I called out: "Now, what have you decided? Are you going or coming? I want to sleep."

The answer soon came in the hoarse voice of someone with a cold: "We're going, you son of a bitch."

And I could hear someone leaving the entrance and squeaking away in the snow.

The expression "son of a bitch" is America's—as well as England's—

national insult. I could not allow myself to be addressed that way without making some sort of reply, and I had an urge to open the door and fire at the scoundrels. I held back, though, thinking at the last minute that possibly just one of the men had left the entryway, while the other perhaps waited for me to open the door so that he could attack me. I therefore went over to one of the windows, sent the roller shade up to the ceiling as quick as lightning, and peeked out. I thought I saw a dark object against the snow. I opened the window, aimed as well as I could at the dark point, and pulled the trigger. Click. I tried again. Click. Furious, I went through the whole cylinder without aiming, and finally a single pitiful shot went off. It made a big bang in that frozen air, and I heard someone over on the road yell: "Run! Run!"

Suddenly a man, still in the entryway, ran out into the snow and disappeared down the road. I had guessed right: there was one of them left. And I could not nicely tell this man good-night, for there had been only the one miserable shot in the revolver, the one I fired.

I lit the lamp again, got out the money, and put it in my pocket. Now that the whole thing was over with, I became such a terrible coward that I did not dare lie down in the couple's bed that night. After waiting a half hour or so, until it began to get light outdoors, I put on my overcoat and left the house, shutting and barring the broken door as best I could. I sneaked down to the town and rang the doorbell at the hotel.

Who the crooks were, I do not know. They were hardly professionals, for if they had been they would not have given up because of a door when there were two windows they could have come through. But neither were these scoundrels without a certain cold and brazen capacity for violence, since they broke both the lock and the prop on the outer door.

Never have I been so fearful for my life as I was that night in the prairie town of Madelia, Jesse James's hideout. Since then, there have also been a couple of times when I was so frightened that my heartbeat worked right up into my throat and made it hard for me to breathe—a reminder of that night. Before that, I had never known of a fright that could have such an extraordinary effect.

On the Prairie

Hamsun found more material for storytelling in Dakota Territory than in any other place where he had resided while in the United States, though he spent much less time there than in Wisconsin or Minnesota. The harshness of life in the Red River Valley seemed to appeal to his sense of the dramatic. The following narrative first appeared in print in 1897.

*T*he whole summer of 1887 I worked on a section of Dalrymple's enormous farm in the Red River Valley of America. Besides me, there were two other Norwegians, a Swede, ten or twelve Irishmen, and some Americans. We were about twenty men altogether in our little group—a mere fraction of the entire farm's hundreds of laborers.

The greenish yellow prairie stretched away as endlessly as a sea. No house was visible, with the exception of our own barns and bunkhouses in the midst of the prairie. No tree, no bush grew there, only wheat and grass, wheat and grass, as far as the eye could reach. There were no flowers, either, nothing but the yellow blossoms of the wild mustard that we came upon now and then in the wheat. Cultivation of mustard was prohibited; we tore it out by the roots, brought it in, and dried and burned it.

And no birds flew. No life could be seen, only the wheat billowing in the wind, and no sound was heard except for the eternal clacking and chirping of the grasshoppers, the prairie's only song.

We had a craving for shade. When the chuck wagon came out to us at noon, we lay on our bellies under it to get a little shade while we tore into the food. The sun was harsh. We wore hats, shirts, trousers, shoes, and nothing more, but we could not wear less or we would burn up. If a hole was torn in the shirt during work, the sun would burn through it and leave a blister on the skin.

During the harvesting of the wheat we worked as long as sixteen hours a day. Every day we drove ten reapers, one after another, through the same field. When one square was completely mowed, we drove into another square and disposed of it. So it went, on and on, while ten men followed us and piled the bundles of wheat up in stacks. And high on his horse, with a revolver in his pocket and with his eyes on the alert, the foreman sat and observed us. Every day he rode his two horses until they were worn out. If something went wrong—if, for example, a machine broke down—the foreman was immediately on the spot and either made the necessary repairs or ordered the machine sent home. He might be far away when he noticed that something was amiss, and since there were few roads, he had to ride around in the thick wheat all day, until the horses would foam with sweat.

When September came, and then October, it was still terribly hot in the daytime, but the nights turned quite cold. We often froze. And we did not get nearly enough sleep, being called out as early as three o'clock in the morning, while it was still dark. Then, when we had fed the horses and ourselves and had driven a long way out to the work place, daybreak would finally arrive and we could see what lay before us. We would set fire to a stack of wheat to thaw out the oilcans that we used to lubricate the machinery, and at the same time we would warm ourselves a bit. But not many minutes passed before we had to be up on the reapers again.

We never had a holiday. Sunday was just like Monday. But when it rained we could do nothing with the wheat, so we stayed in, played casino, chatted with one another, and slept.

One of the Irishmen made quite an impression on me at the outset. God knows what he was originally. In rainy weather he always lay and read novels that he had brought with him. He was a big, handsome fellow, about thirty-six years old, and he spoke exquisite English. He also knew German.

This man had come to the farm in a silk shirt, and he continued to work in silk shirts the whole time. When one of them wore out, he put on a new one. He was not a very skillful worker—he had poor coordination, a lack of manual dexterity—but he was an extraordinary man. His name was Evans.

There was nothing special about the two Norwegians. One of them, from Hallingdal, left because he could not keep up the work; the other, from Valdres, stayed on.

During the threshing we all tried to get a position as far away from the steam-powered thresher as possible, because a blizzard of dust, sand, and chaff arose from all the blades and orifices of the machine. For several days I was in the midst of this storm, so I asked the foreman to shift me to something else, which he did. He gave me an excellent place out in the field, where I was to help load the wagons. He never forgot the favor that I had done him right at the beginning.

It happened like this: My jacket with its shiny buttons was part of the uniform left over from the time when I was a streetcar conductor in Chicago. The jacket and its superb buttons appealed to the foreman, who was a veritable child when it came to fancy clothes, which he could not obtain out there on the prairie. One day I told him he was welcome to the jacket. He wanted to pay me for it and asked me to name my price. When I gave it to him as a gift, he declared that he owed me a great debt of gratitude. And when the harvesting was over he presented me with another jacket, a good one, seeing that I had none to travel in.

I remember the following incident from those days when I worked at loading wheat on the wagons: The Swede came after a load. He had on some big boots with his pant legs tucked in the tops. We were in the process of loading. He was a very devil for work, and I had all I could do to keep up with him. Faster and faster he went, and when this began to annoy me I also speeded up.

Each stack of wheat consisted of eight bundles, and as a rule we took only one bundle at a time and tossed it up on the load. Now I took four. I inundated the Swede with bundles, overwhelmed him with bundles. It turned out that a snake went along with one of the heavy armfuls that I sent up to the Swede. It slithered down into one of his boots. I did not notice anything until I suddenly heard a terrible scream and saw the Swede jump down from the load with the dark-spotted snake dangling out of his boot top. It did not bite him, and when he hit the ground the snake pulled out of the boot and disappeared down the field as quick as lightning. Both of us went after it with our hayforks but could not find it. The two mules that were hitched to the wagon stood there and shook.

I can still hear the Swede's scream and see him in midair as he threw himself off the load.

After that, we agreed that in the future he would work at a more reasonable pace and I would send him only one bundle of wheat at a time.

Having plowed and sown, cut and harvested the hay, reaped and threshed the wheat, we were finally through—and were paid off. With glad hearts and money in our pockets, we tramped, twenty men strong, down to the nearest prairie town to find a train that would take us back East again. The foreman went along with us, wearing the jacket with the shiny buttons, to drink a beaker with us at our farewell party.

If you have never taken part in such a farewell party with a crew of prairie farm laborers, you can hardly imagine how wild a binge it turns into. Everybody immediately gives a round of drinks—which comes to twenty glasses per man. But if you think it ends with this, you are mistaken, for verily there are gentlemen among us who order five rounds at once. And God pity the barkeeper who would object to such excess, for he would promptly be thrown out of his own bar. Such a gang of summer workers will toss down all that comes their way. By the fifth toast to the prominent townsmen present, they throw up, and from then on they frolic without restraint. The local police are powerless; they join the gang and drink with us. And the drinking, playing, pouring, and hollering goes on for at least a couple of days and nights.

We workers became extremely amiable. Throughout the summer we had often been rather indifferent toward one another, but now with our leave-taking all unfriendliness was forgotten. As we drank we gradually grew more and more bighearted, serving one another until we nearly collapsed and, quite emotional, fell into each other's arms. The cook, a hunchbacked little man with a woman's voice and no beard, hiccuping in Norwegian, confided to me that he too was a Norseman, just like me, and the only reason he had not acknowledged it was the Yankees' general contempt for Norwegians. He had often overheard the Valdres man and me talking about him during meals, and he had understood every word, but now he was willing to forget and forgive us, since we were such gorgeous boys. Yes, indeed, he "was born to one of Old Norway's brave sons, was born in Iowa the 22nd of July, 1845." And therefore we must be good friends and partners as long as the Norwegian language flowed from our lips. The cook and I embraced, agreeing that our friendship would never end. All the workers embraced one another, hugging with their hardened arms and dancing around in their enthusiasm.

We would say to each other: "What would you like to drink now? There's nothing around here that's good enough for you." And then we would step behind the bar ourselves to look for the most delicious beverages. From high up on the shelves we took down some interesting bottles, beautifully labeled bottles that stood there mainly for show. We good friends poured out the contents for one another, drank it up, and paid ridiculously high prices for it.

Evans was undoubtedly the worst at ordering fresh rounds. The last of his silk shirts now had a sorry look, its gaudy colors faded from sun and rain, its sleeves ragged. But Evans himself stood tall and proud and ordered the rounds with authority. He owned the saloon, he owned the world. The rest of us usually paid about three dollars for a round, but Evans asked right out whether he could not get different rounds for six dollars. For, said he, in all this miserable shack there was nothing good enough for such gentlemen as he had with him here. It was then that we had to resort to the remarkable bottles up on the shelves to find something expensive enough.

In his tipsy friendliness, Evans took me aside and tried to persuade me to go with him down into the Wisconsin forest and cut cordwood during the winter. Once he had outfitted himself with some new shirts, a pair of pants, and a few new novels, he was going into the woods and staying there until spring, he said. And when spring came he would look for a place out on the prairie again. This was his life. For twelve years he had divided his time between the forest and the prairie, and he had gotten so used to it that now it was automatic.

But when I asked him what had led him into such a career in the first place, he did not answer—as drunk people often do—with a long, elaborate, rambling exposition, but only with the single word: "Circumstances."

"How?" I asked.

"Circumstances!" he repeated. And he would say no more about it.

Later in the evening I saw him in a side room of the saloon where they were shooting craps. Evans had lost. He was fairly drunk and not concerned about the money. When I went in he showed me a single bill and said: "I still have money. See!"

Several bystanders advised him to quit the game. One of his countrymen, an Irishman by the name of O'Brien, suggested that he ought to save his folding money for the train ticket. Evans was offended. "No," he said. "You can lend me travel money."

O'Brien curtly refused and left the room. Now Evans was really provoked. He promptly bet all his bills and lost them. Taking it calmly, he lit a cigar, smiled, and said to me: "Will you lend me travel money?"

I was a bit dizzy as a result of drinking the vile stuff from one of those bottles on the high shelves. Unbuttoning my jacket, I took out my wallet and handed it, with all that was in it, to Evans. I meant to show him that I was ready and willing to lend him the travel money and that I was leaving it up to him to take what he needed. He looked at me, then at the wallet. He seemed strangely moved as he opened the wallet and saw that it contained all my money. When he looked at me again, I merely nodded.

He misunderstood this nod. He assumed that I was giving him the whole amount. "Thank you," he said.

And to my great alarm he put up some of my money on another throw of the dice. I wanted to stop him, but held back. Let him use his travel money any way he wants, I thought. But when he has gambled away a reasonable amount, I will take back the rest.

Evans was no longer losing, though. Suddenly sober, he was rolling the dice quickly and decisively. Apparently he had been transformed by the confidence his comrades who were present showed in him. Sitting still and straight on the whiskey keg that served as a chair, he kept putting in and taking out his winnings. Whenever he lost, he doubled his stake the next time. He lost three times in a row, doubled every time, and at last won it all back. Then he put in a whole five-dollar bill and said that if he won he would now quit.

He lost. And he kept on playing.

After an hour had gone by, he gave me back my wallet with the money in it; he had kept an exact account all through the game. Once more he had a whole pile of bills for himself. He played on. Suddenly he put in all he possessed. A murmur went through the room from those of us who were looking on.

Evans said: "Win or lose, I'm now going to quit."

He won. Getting up, he said to the game's banker: "Please pay me."

"Tomorrow," the banker replied. "I don't have it tonight. I'll settle with you tomorrow."

Evans said: "Okay, tomorrow then."

We were about to leave when some men came tramping heavily into the room. They were carrying a dismembered body. It was the Irishman O'Brien, the one who had refused to lend Evans travel money. He had just been run over by a wheat train, and both of his legs were cut off, one of them clear up at the thigh. He was already dead. From our room he had gone out into the dark and staggered right in under the wheels of a train. The body was laid on the floor and covered up.

Then we looked wherever we could for a place to sleep. Some lay down on the floor of the saloon itself, while the Valdres man and I found us a barn out in the town.

The next morning Evans came down the street.

"Have you got your money from the banker?" asked my friend from Valdres.

"Not yet," Evans answered. "I've been out in the field digging a hole for our comrade."

Not far from town we buried O'Brien in a box we had taken out of a house, a box that happened to be long enough, the body having been cut so short. We neither sang nor prayed, but we gathered around and stood for a moment with our hats in our hands. Then the ceremony was over.

When Evans tried to get the money he had won, it turned out that the wily banker had disappeared. Evens took this with his usual calm, seeming to be quite indifferent about it. After all, he had a lot of money left, more than enough to pay for his railroad ticket and his shirts, pants, and novels. And then he would be equipped for the winter.

We stayed in town until the next afternoon, carrying on as before and drinking the saloon dry. By the time we left the place, several of the workers were flat broke, and since they could not afford railroad tickets, they smuggled themselves into freight cars, where they buried themselves in the wheat. But the old hunchbacked cook, that Norwegian from Iowa, bungled his attempt. He was lucky enough to get into the wheat without being seen, but once he was there he could not keep still, and drunkenly he began to sing lewd ditties in his womanish voice. Consequently he was discovered and thrown out. And when the little man was searched, he had so much money on him that he could easily have paid the fare for all of us, the scoundrel!

We scattered to the four winds. The man from Valdres bought a little shooting gallery in a Minnesota town, and the cook moved out West to the Pacific Coast. But Evans is, without doubt, still going around in his silk shirts and handing out money carelessly. Every summer he is out there on the prairie harvesting wheat, and every winter he is in the Wisconsin woods chopping timber. This is his life.

That kind of life may be just as good as any other.

Zachæus

Of Hamsun's narratives based on his American experiences, this is the only one told in the third person, without his appearing as a participant and narrator. Like some other writings in this collection, "Zachæus" shows his fascination if not preoccupation with Irish Americans. It was originally published in 1899.

I

*T*he most profound peace lies over the prairie. For miles around, no trees or houses can be seen, only wheat and green grass as far as the eye can reach. Far, far away, looking as small as flies, are horses and people at work, haymakers sitting on their machines and mowing the grass in strips. The only sounds to be heard are the chirp of the grasshoppers and, on rare occasions when the breeze is right, the clacking noise of the mowing machines out on the horizon. Sometimes this noise sounds strangely near.

The place is Billybony Farm. It lies all alone in the wide West, without neighbors, without any connection to the rest of the world, several days' march from the nearest little prairie town. From a distance its buildings look like tiny rock islands in the boundless sea of wheat. The farm is not inhabited during the winter, but from spring to late October there are seventy-odd men working at the place. There are three men in the kitchen, the cook and his two helpers, and there are twenty jackasses in the barn, but no women, not a solitary woman on Billybony Farm.

In the glow of the sun it is 102 degrees Fahrenheit, sky and earth continually quiver in the heat, and no real breath of wind cools the air. The sun looks like a morass of fire.

All is quiet at the home buildings except that at the large, crude, shingle-roofed structure used for a kitchen and mess hall one can hear the voices and footsteps of the cook and his assistants as they bustle about. They use hay for fuel in the huge cookstove, and sparks and flames mingle with the smoke as it streams up the chimney. When the food is ready the three men carry it out in zinc tubs and load it on wagons, then hitch up the jackasses and drive out on the prairie with it.

The cook is a big Irishman, forty years old, gray-headed, with a military bearing. He is half-naked, his shirt open, and his chest like a millstone. Everybody calls him Polly, because he has a face like a parrot's.

Polly has been a soldier, stationed at one of the forts down South. He is literate, can read, and has with him a songbook and, besides that, an old issue of a newspaper. These jewels he will let nobody touch. He keeps them on a shelf in the kitchen, so as to have them at hand during his free moments. And he makes diligent use of them.

But Zachæus, his wretched countryman, who is nearly blind and wears glasses, once took possession of the newspaper to read in it. There was no point in offering Zachæus an ordinary book, with small letters that would run together in a mist for him. However, it was a real pleasure for him to hold the cook's newspaper in his hands and dwell on the advertisements with their large print. But the cook immediately missed his treasure, found Zachæus in bed, and took the paper away from him. Then a violent and comical argument erupted between the two men.

The cook called Zachæus a blackhearted robber and a son of a bitch. Snapping his fingers under Zachæus's nose, he asked whether he had ever seen a soldier and whether he knew the layout of a fort. No, of course not! He had better watch himself, by God, and keep his mouth shut! How much did he make a month? Did he own property in Washington, and had his cow calved yesterday?

Zachæus gave no answer to these questions, but accused the cook of serving meat that was raw and bread pudding that had flies in it. The cook could go to hell and take the newspaper with him. He—Zachæus—was an honorable man and would have put the paper back after studying it. "So don't stand there and spit on the floor, you dirty dog!" And in Zachæus's angry face his blind eyes stood out like two hard steel balls.

From that day on, there was constant hostility between the two countrymen.

The wagons with food go their separate ways out over the prairie, each of them providing meals for twenty-five men. The people come running from all directions, grab some food, and throw themselves under the wagons so as to get a bit of shade while eating. In ten minutes the food is consumed, the foreman sits in the saddle ordering the people back to work, and the chuck wagons head back to the mess hall.

After the midday meal, while the cook's helpers wash and dry the dishes, Polly himself sits out in the shade behind the building and, for the thousandth time, reads his songs and soldier ballads in the precious book that he has kept with him since he was in that fort down South. And now Polly is a soldier again.

II

In the evening, when it is already dark, seven hayracks roll slowly in from the prairie with the workforce. Most of the men wash their hands out in the yard before they go in for the evening meal, and some also comb their hair. They are of various ages and national backgrounds, young and old, immigrants from Europe and native-born Americans, nearly all of them homeless drifters and most of them rascals.

The better-off among them carry a revolver in their hip pocket. All eat in a great hurry, without taking time to talk. They respect the foreman, who eats with them and maintains order. And as soon as they finish eating they go to bed.

But now was the time that Zachæus chose to wash his shirt. It had become so stiff with dried sweat that it chafed him during the day, when he felt the broiling sun on his back. The night was quite dark, and the only thing that could be heard was the sound of muffled conversation that came from the big bunkhouse.

Zachæus went over to the kitchen wall, where there were several rain barrels. These contained the rainwater that the cook painstakingly collected because the well water was too hard, too full of lime, to wash in. The night was cold and Zachæus practically froze, but his shirt had to be laundered, and he whistled to keep his spirits up.

Suddenly the cook opened the kitchen door. He held a lamp in his hand, and a broad beam of light fell on Zachæus.

"Aha!" said the cook as he came out.

He set the lamp down on the step, went right up to Zachæus, and demanded: "Who gave you that water?"

"I took it," Zachæus replied.

"That's my water!" Polly screamed. "And you have taken it, you liar, thief, and son of a bitch."

Zachæus made no further reply, but merely began to repeat his accusation about flies in the pudding.

The two fellows were making so much racket that it attracted people from the bunkhouse, who stood around in knots and, with the greatest interest, listened to the exchange of words.

Polly yelled to them: "Isn't that nice of the worthless, no-good pig? My own water!"

"Take your water!" said Zachæus as he tipped the barrel over. "I'm through with it."

The cook stuck his fist under Zachæus's eyes and asked: "Do you see that?"

"Yes," answered Zachæus.

"I'm going to let you taste it."

"If you dare."

All at once there was the sound of some quick blows being given and taken. The onlookers let out yell after yell to express their approval and enjoyment.

But Zachæus did not hold out very long. The squat, dim-sighted Irishman was desperate as a lemming, but his arms were much too short for him to keep on against the cook. At last he tottered three or four steps sideways and then keeled over.

The cook addressed the crowd: "Okay, there he lies. Let him lie. A soldier has felled him."

"I think he's dead," said a voice.

The cook shrugged his shoulders. "Very well!" he responded indifferently. And in front of his audience he felt like a great, invincible, victorious lord. He threw back his head and, to emphasize his self-esteem, he waxed literary.

"The hell with him," he said. "Let him lie there. Does he think he's Daniel Webster? He comes along and tries to tell me how to make pudding—me, who has cooked for generals! I ask you, is he a colonel in command of the prairie?"

And they could not help admiring Polly's speech.

Now Zachæus raised himself off the ground and, still defiant, said angrily: "Come on, you cowardly rabbit!"

The crowd roared with delight, but the cook answered with a pitying smile: "Nonsense! I could just as easily be beaten by this lamp." With that, he picked up the lamp and slowly and self-importantly went inside.

Now that the place was dark, the men made their way back to the bunkhouse. As for Zachæus, he took his shirt, wrung it out thoroughly, and put it on. Then he sauntered after the others to find his bunk and go to sleep.

III

Out on the prairie the next day Zachæus knelt in the grass oiling his machine. The sun was as hot as usual, and sweat ran down his eyes behind his glasses. Suddenly the horses jerked ahead a couple of steps, either frightened by something or stung by an insect. Zachæus let out a shriek and jumped high off the ground. In a little while he began to wave his left hand in the air and to chase back and forth.

A man operating a hay rake nearby stopped his horse and asked: "What's the matter?"

Zachæus replied: "Come here a minute and help me."

When the man came Zachæus showed him a bloody hand and said: "My finger has been cut off; it happened just now. Look for the finger; I can't see."

The man searched for the finger and found it in the grass. There were two joints of it. It was already beginning to shrivel and looked like a tiny corpse.

Zachæus took the finger, examined it, and remarked: "Yeah, that's it. Wait a while; hold on to it for a minute."

Drawing his shirt up out of his pants, Zachæus tore two strips off it. With one of them he bandaged his hand, and with the other he wrapped up his severed finger, which he stuck in his pocket. Then, thanking his comrade for the help, he seated himself on his machine.

He held out almost until evening. As soon as the foreman heard about his accident, he bawled him out and sent him home to the farm.

The first thing Zachæus did was to preserve his severed finger. Though he had no alcohol, he kept machine oil in a bottle, and he slipped the finger into it and corked it up. He put the bottle under the sack of straw in his bunk.

For a whole week he stayed home, as his hand grew intensely painful and he had to lie there holding it still night and day. His head throbbed, his body was racked with fever, and he suffered and fretted inordinately. Such prolonged inactivity he had never experienced before, not even that time several years ago when the mine blast went off and damaged his eyes.

To make his miserable condition even worse, Polly the cook brought his meals to his bedside every day and took advantage of the opportunity to bedevil the invalid. The two enemies got into many good quarrels during this period, and more than once Zachæus had to turn his face to the wall and bite his tongue because he was so overmatched in the battle.

Meanwhile the painful nights and days came and went with unendurable slowness. As soon as possible Zachæus began to sit up in his bunk a little, and during the heat of the day he kept the door open to the prairie and the sky. Often he sat with his mouth open, listening for the sound of the reapers far, far away, and talking aloud to his horses as if they were right in front of him.

But the malicious Polly, the scheming Polly, still could not leave him alone. He would come and slam the door behind him on the pretext that there was a draft, a terrible draft, which he could not put up with. Then Zachæus would tumble out of his bunk and throw a boot or a stool at the cook, always with the serious intention of crippling him for life. No such luck. Zachæus, with his poor eyesight, could not aim straight, and he never hit the target.

On the seventh day he declared that he was going to eat the noon meal in the kitchen. The cook answered that he absolutely refused to permit such a visit. So, once again, Zachæus had to accept the meal in his bunk. He sat there all forlorn, getting angrier and angrier in his boredom. The kitchen, he knew, was now empty, the cook and his helpers being out on the prairie with the midday meal. He had heard them leave; they were singing and hollering just to gloat over the shut-in.

Zachæus stepped out of the bunk and staggered over to the kitchen. He looked around, found the book and the newspaper lying in their usual place, picked up the paper, and staggered back to the bunkhouse. Then, wiping his glasses, he began to read the delightfully big letters in the advertisements.

An hour passed, then two hours—time went so fast now. Finally Zachæus heard the chuck wagons come back, and he heard the voice of the cook, who, as usual, was telling his helpers to wash the dishes.

Zachæus realized that the paper would be missed the moment the cook went to his library. After a second's thought he stuck the paper under the straw sack in the bunk. A little later he hastily took the paper out and put it next to his bare skin. Never in his life would he give it up again!

A minute passed. Then heavy steps could be heard coming toward the bunkhouse. Zachæus lay on his back and stared at the ceiling. Polly walked in.

"Where is it? Have you got my paper?" he asked, standing in the middle of the floor.

"No," answered Zachæus.

"You do, too, have it," the cook hissed and moved closer to him.

Zachæus sat up. "I don't have your paper," he said angrily. "Go to hell!"

The cook now threw the sick man out on the floor and began to search the bunk. He turned over the straw sack and checked the ragged blanket several times without finding what he was looking for.

"You've got it," he insisted. After he had left and was out in the yard he turned around and repeated: "You took it. But wait, my good friend!"

With a blend of malice and self-satisfaction, Zachæus laughed at him and said: "Okay, I took it. I had use for it, you dirty dog."

The cook's parrot-face turned red as a beet, and his expression was as scary as a fire alarm. He looked back at Zachæus and muttered: "Just wait!"

IV

The next day was stormy, with pouring rain that pelted the houses like hail and filled the cook's barrels by early morning. All the workers stayed indoors, some of them mending wheat sacks for the harvest, others repairing broken tools and implements or sharpening mowing-machine blades.

When the dinner call sounded, Zachæus got up from the bunk where he was sitting and started to go along with the others to the mess hall. Right outside the door, however, he was met by Polly, who was bringing him his meal. Zachæus objected that he had decided to eat together with the rest from now on. His hand was better, he said, and he no longer had any fever. The cook answered that Zachæus would take what was brought him or he would not get anything at all. Then, flinging the tin dish down on the bunk, the cook asked:

"Isn't it good enough for you?"

Zachæus went back to his bunk and gave up. He had better take whatever food he could get. So he started to eat, growling: "What kind of pig slop have you cooked today?"

"Chicken," the cook replied. And there was a peculiar gleam in his eyes as he turned around and went out.

"Chicken?" Zachæus mumbled to himself and examined the food with his semiblind eyes. "Like hell it is, you liar! But it's meat and gravy."

And he ate some of the meat.

Suddenly he got a piece in his mouth that he could not identify. He could not bite into it. It was a bone with shriveled meat on it, and after he had gnawed on one side of it, he took it out of his mouth and looked at it. "The dirty dog can keep the bone to himself," he muttered as he went to the door to examine it more closely. He turned it over several times. Suddenly he hurried back to the bunk and looked for the bottle with the severed finger in it. The bottle was gone.

Zachæus walked over to the mess hall. Pale as a cadaver, his face distorted, he stood inside the door and said to the cook, in the hearing of everybody:

"Listen, Polly, isn't this my finger?"

With that, he held up the little thing.

The cook did not answer, but began to snicker over at his table.

Holding up another little object, Zachæus asked: "And, Polly, isn't this the nail that was on my finger? Do you recognize it?"

Now all the men at the tables were paying close attention to the peculiar questions from Zachæus and looking at him with amazement.

"What's the matter?" one of them asked.

"I found my finger, my cut-off finger, in the food," Zachæus explained. "He went and cooked it; he gave it to me in my grub. Here's the nail, too."

A roar of laughter went up from the tables, and the men all began talking at the same time.

"He's cooked and given you your own finger? You bit into it, you say, and you chewed on one side of it?"

"I can't see very well," Zachæus answered. "I didn't know . . . I didn't think . . . " Then he shut up, turned around, and went out the door.

The foreman had to restore order in the mess hall. He got up, turned to the cook, and asked: "Did you cook that finger along with the rest of the meat, Polly?"

"No," Polly replied. "Good God, no. What kind of a man do you take me for? I cooked it separately, in a completely different pot."

All afternoon the story of the cooked finger remained an inexhaustible source of fun for the gang. They discussed it and laughed about it as if they were crazy, and the cook enjoyed a triumph like none before in all his life. But Zachæus had disappeared.

Zachæus had gone out on the prairie. The storm continued, and there was no shelter to be found anywhere, but he wandered farther and farther out. He had his hurt hand in a bandage and protected it as well as he could from the rain. Except for that, he was sopping wet from head to toe.

He kept on walking. When it began to get dark he looked at his watch in the light of a lightning flash and started back the same way he had come. He walked through the wheat with slow, deliberate steps as if he had carefully calculated the time and the speed. By eight o'clock he was back home at the farm.

It was now completely dark. He could hear the sound of people at supper in the mess hall, and when he peeked in the window he thought he saw the cook in an excellent mood.

He walked away from the building, over to the barn, where he stood under shelter and stared out into the darkness. The grasshoppers were silent; all was quiet, but the rain kept on pouring down, and now and then sulphur-colored lightning streaked across the sky and struck the prairie far away.

Finally Zachæus heard the people leaving the mess hall and heading for the bunkhouse, cursing and making a mad dash for it, trying to keep from getting wet. Patiently, determinedly, he waited an hour longer, then set out toward the kitchen.

There was still a light inside. He could see a man at the stove, and calmly walking in he greeted him: "Good evening."

The cook gave him a surprised look, then finally said: "You can't have any food this evening."

Zachæus answered: "Okay. But give me a little soap, Polly. I didn't get my shirt clean yesterday afternoon, and I need to wash it again."

"Not in my water," said the cook.

"Yes, indeed. I have it right here, around the corner."

"I'd advise you against that."

"Do I get the soap?" Zachæus asked.

"I'll give you soap," the cook replied. "Get out of here!"

And Zachæus went out. He took one of the barrels, moved it to the corner right under the kitchen window, and began to splash violently in the water.

Hearing this, the cook came out, as puffed up and arrogant as ever. With his sleeves rolled up, he went over to Zachæus and irately demanded: "What are you doing here?"

Zachæus replied: "Nothing. Just washing my shirt."

"In my water?"

"Of course."

The cook came closer, bent over the barrel to identify it, and felt in the water for the shirt.

Then Zachæus drew his revolver out of the bandage on his injured hand, stuck it right in the cook's ear, and pulled the trigger.

Only a faint report could be heard in the moist night.

V

Late that night, when Zachæus entered the bunkhouse to go to bed, a couple of his comrades woke up in their bunks. They asked what he had been doing outside for so long.

Zachæus answered: "Nothing. Except I shot Polly."

The comrades raised up on their elbows to hear better.

"You shot him?"

"Yeah."

"The hell you did! Where did you hit him?"

"In the head. I shot him through the ear, upward."

"Well, I'll be damned! Where did you bury him?"

"West of here, on the prairie. I laid the newspaper between his hands."

"You did!"

The comrades lay back down to go to sleep. After a while one of them, still awake, asked: "Did he die right away?"

"Yeah," answered Zachæus, "almost. The bullet went through his brain."

"Yeah, that's the best kind of a shot," said the comrade. "If it goes through the brain, it means death."

Then the building became quiet and everyone slept.

Next morning the foreman had to appoint a new cook. He picked one of the old assistants, who was secretly happy about the murder.

All went their ways to the harvest. There was no further talk about Polly's passing. The poor devil was dead, lying in the wheat someplace where a small patch of it had been disturbed. There was nothing more to be done about the matter.

When October came the Billybony workers went down to the nearest town to drink together before separating. At this moment all were better friends than ever before, and they heartily embraced and bought drinks for one another.

"Where do you go from here, Zachæus?"

"I'm going to travel a little farther west," Zachæus replied. "To Wyoming, maybe. But by winter I'll take to the logging forest again."

"Well, we may meet there. So long till then, Zachæus. Have a good trip!"

The comrades scattered in all directions, out into the vast Yankeeland. Zachæus went to Wyoming.

And the prairie lies like a boundless sea, upon which the October sun shines with long beams that look like awls.

Vagabond Days

*Tramp life, of which Hamsun writes in this piece, was in his time a recent phe-
nomenon in the United States, having its origin in the depression of the 1870s.
By unintentionally providing free rides, the railroads made the new vagrancy
possible, and by providing transportation for the harvested wheat, made possible the bonanza farms with their opportunities for seasonal employment. In this
story, published in 1904–1905, as in the later "My First Time Abroad," the author pictures himself as something of a loser, one who is taken advantage of and
fails to get the girl. While most of the scenes are set on the Dakota prairie, the
town of Eliot, where the bank robbery occurs, is based on Elroy, Wisconsin, as
Harald S. Næss has indicated.*

I

"*U*p, folks!" cried the foreman in charge of Orange Flat section. We could
not see him, for it was still dark and chilly, three o'clock in the morning,
but we promptly leapt out of our beds and put on our shirts and pants.

It was harvest time and we were working like dogs, never getting enough
sleep. All of us were in an unnaturally excited state. We quarreled with one
another over little things, and when, in the course of the day, we ran into
the slightest resistance in our work, we used force and broke our implements.

The foreman himself, as hard as nails, had grown thin. He told us the
neighboring section had got far ahead and would finish harvesting several
days before us. "That must never happen!" we replied, gritting our teeth.
We meant to catch up with the neighboring section, yes, to pass it in a flash,
and no one was going to stop us. That was why the foreman had been call-

ing us out at three in the morning for the past two weeks. "Up, folks!" he would yell again at three tomorrow and the day after tomorrow. We could see no end to this mad rush.

We hurried in to breakfast and forced ourselves to gobble the barest essentials of bread and butter, meat and coffee. It was good meat, but we no longer had any appetite. In ten minutes we would be sitting on the wagons and riding out to the field to work.

And we would labor like completely crazy creatures. We knew very well that praise and recognition awaited us if we could get even a single day ahead of the neighboring section, which also was making the uttermost effort. Everybody has his ambition in this world, and we had ours.

Dawn came, the sun rose and began to glow, and we threw off our shirts. Hundreds of men were spread out over the endless wheat prairie. And there we would swarm back and forth until dark.

"I don't know whether I can stand this any longer, Noot," said Huntley, the Irishman.

And "Noot," that's me.

Later in the day I heard that Huntley had said the same thing to the tramp Jess—that he could not stand it any more.

I started in on him about his blabbermouth and bawled him out for saying what he did to a tramp.

Huntley understood well enough that he thereby had got some power over me, had aroused my jealousy. He spoke out even more, declaring openly:

"I'm not putting up with this any longer. I'm clearing out tonight. If you want to go with me, I will be at the north corner of the barn at twelve o'clock."

"I'm not going with you," I said.

I thought about it all day as I worked, and when evening came I was still determined not to go along with Huntley. I realized that he would have a chance to talk to me about it during the evening meal and later when we went to bed, but meanwhile I avoided him and remained confident that I could resist him.

That night the men undressed and went to bed. All was dark. Several minutes later the whole room was snoring.

With my clothes still on, I sat on my bed thinking. In a few hours the foreman would yell "Up, folks!" and the day would be just like the last one.

But it was probably no more than a two days' hike from here to a farm or town where I could find other work and earn a living. And I might be able to get more sleep there.

I sneaked out of the room and went over to the north corner of the barn.

Huntley was already there, standing hunched up with his back against the wall and his hands in his pockets. He was freezing. In a little while the tramp Jess arrived.

I asked: "Is Jess going along, too?"

"Certainly," Huntley answered. "Just him. You didn't want to."

"Yes, I do," I said, wanting to be off right away.

"Well, it's too late now," Huntley declared. "I don't have provisions for more than us two."

Getting angry, I said: "Then I'll report you to the foreman."

"You will?" Huntley asked softly, very softly. Then he said: "No, you won't. Absolutely not."

He had come up so close to me that I could feel his breath.

"Hold it," whispered the tramp. "If Noot wants to come along I can find some more food. I know where the cook has some meat stored."

While Jess the tramp was away, Huntley and I stood by the barn and quarreled over my having said I would tell on him, and when Jess came back with the meat Huntley was still infuriated. He said:

"Couldn't you find any more meat, you no-account! What good is that for a grown man? Well, here is your meat, Noot," he said as he tossed it to me.

Then we sneaked away from Orange Flat.

II

We set out in a northerly direction, to look for the closest railroad track, and we walked for a couple of hours. Then Jess the tramp declared that he had to get a little sleep, though Huntley and I could have kept going for a while longer.

There was prairie on every side, and no sign of morning. Since it was a frosty night, we had made our way through the wheat fields and the prairie grass without getting wet. We now circled around a couple of times, feeling ahead with our feet to find a good place to lie down. I lay on my elbows and dozed with my head in my hands.

Suddenly Jess woke us. He must have slept so little in recent weeks that he could not go to sleep now. "Up, folks!" he called.

Sleepy and confused, we jumped up, but there was no danger, only peace and darkness all around us. Huntley, cursing, insisted that it had not been necessary to call us yet.

Jess answered: "Let's see if we can't go farther. With so much white frost everywhere, the foreman can follow our tracks right from the barn, and anyone riding a pony can easily catch up with us."

"So what?" demanded Huntley. "We'll kill him."

"He can shoot us first," Jess replied.

So we started north again. On our right it looked as if the sky was beginning to brighten. Our little nap had done us good, raising our spirits a bit. Even Jess, who had not slept, seemed to have gotten more energy. He walked with a livelier step than before and stumbled less often on the uneven prairie ground.

"By now they are awake back at the section," said Jess. He could tell by the way the sky looked. A little later he said: "Now they are eating breakfast. Now he's asking about us."

Involuntarily we all walked faster.

"Now he's out looking for us," Jess said.

I could hear my heart beating.

"Shut your mouth!" Huntley exclaimed. "Can't you talk less or, better yet, keep quiet?"

"He'll have to ride pretty fast if he's going to catch us now," I said, to cheer things up.

"You're right about that," Huntley agreed. "He'll never get near us."

Huntley's confidence grew. Soon we could hear him beginning surreptitiously to eat some of the provisions he was carrying.

The sky became lighter and lighter. When the sun came up, Jess stopped and looked back. There was nothing to see, no rider, not a living thing. Nor was there a house or a tree anywhere on that boundless sea of a prairie.

Jess said: "Now we will lay our course a couple of points to the east. Pretty soon the sun will thaw the frost and hide our tracks, but if we keep going in the same direction as we have been, the foreman will still be able to catch us."

"You're right about that," Huntley said again. "Let him just keep riding toward the north and he won't find us."

We walked on for a good hour yet, until we were all about to collapse. After sunrise it got warmer and warmer, finally drying the frost and our tracks out of the grass. It must have been seven or eight in the morning when the three of us lay down to rest.

We were so overtired that we could not sleep. I sat straight up and looked at my two companions. Jess the tramp was dark-complected and slim, with small, supple hands and narrow shoulders. God only knows what jobs he may have had and given up to roam, constantly roam, and live the casual life of a tramp. He must have been a sailor at one time, to judge by his knowledge of the compass, his talking about our laying our course two points to the east. Since he knew something about business and merchandise, he may have been connected with a shop in some city. Anyhow, he was a helpful comrade. When he pretended to be tired during the night, it was to get Huntley and me to sleep a little; he stayed awake himself.

Huntley, a much bigger and brawnier man, seemed to have had bad luck. One rainy day at the farm, when we were all idle and chatting, he movingly told how sorry he felt for the man "who has an unfaithful wife." "If you don't love her, then shoot her!" he said, "but if you do love her, then be sad about her all your life and turn into a piece of wreckage and trash!" Apparently he had seen better days. Now undoubtedly an alcoholic, he thought like a sly fox. There was something horrible and repulsive about his eyes. Under his jacket he always wore an old silk shirt that had turned as brown as his skin. It was such a close match that, at first glance, he appeared to be naked from the waist up. Since he was so much stronger than the rest of us, we all had great respect for him.

At last the sun had its effect on me, making me sleepy. And the breeze rustled in the tall grass.

III

It was a very restless sleep. A couple of times I jumped up and screamed, then relaxed and lay back down when I realized where I was. Jess said each time: "Sleep some more, Noot."

Toward morning, when I woke up, my two companions were sitting there eating. They were talking about how we had run away from our wages, how we had slaved on the farm for four weeks without getting any pay.

"When I think about it, I feel like going back and burning down the farm," said Huntley.

He ate freely of his provisions, without saving enough for later. Having my own meat, I only needed some bread, which I also got from Jess. From now on, he and I each had our own supply.

After we had eaten we set out anew. The sun was not yet up; we estimated the time to be four or half past four. And once more we headed north in search of the railroad line.

We kept going until nightfall, then went to bed on the prairie again. Having eaten up the last of his food, Huntley was well-filled when he went to sleep. During the night all three of us woke up from time to time because of the icy cold. Then we ran back and forth in the dark until we fell on our faces in the frosty grass. And creeping close to one another, our teeth chattering, we dozed off and on. Huntley suffered less from the cold than Jess or I because he was so well-fed.

Finally Jess got up and said: "We might just as well walk until the sun comes up. Then we can lie down."

But when we were about to start, Huntley wanted to go one way and Jess another. There was no light, nor were there any stars to guide us.

"I'm going with Jess," I said, and began to walk.

Huntley followed us, swearing and cursing me in particular as a damn fool and a no-good.

When it got light, we began to eat breakfast as we walked along. Huntley, having no food left, walked behind us without a word. By daybreak we were feeling thirsty, and Jess said: "We may not be able to find any water all day, so save your tobacco, boys, and take only a little bit at a time."

But Huntley had used up his tobacco, too, and so we had to share a little of ours with him.

That evening, when it was so dark we could no longer see, we heard the roar of a railroad train far ahead. The sound was music to our ears, and we pushed on with renewed energy. Finally we stumbled upon the rails. But except for the rails there was nothing to be seen either to the east or to the west, so we had to bed down right there and wait until morning. My companions lay on the track itself, with their heads on a rail, but I was not that daring. Having no courage left, I lay in the grass again. And this night, too, came to an end, though I spent most of the time running up and down the track to keep warm.

At dawn Jess suddenly got up and said: "Watch out, boys. Here comes a train."

While lying with his head on the rail, he had felt the weak, distant vibration. We were prepared, and when the train came we signaled the engineer to stop, even though we had no money. Huntley, the fox, knelt and raised his hands, palms together, as if praying to God. But the train roared on past. A wheat train, it could just as well have picked us up. Instead, two sooty men stood in the locomotive laughing at us.

Huntley, standing up, was furious. He said: "I used to have a revolver. Too bad I don't have it any more."

We headed toward the west on the railroad track. It was tough going over the thousands of ties—like walking on a ladder laid flat. Jess and I ate a few mouthfuls. Huntley, having no shame, asked us for a bite but we gave him nothing. And to keep the rest of my food from falling into Huntley's hands while I slept, I ate it all up right in front of him.

"Do you think that was very nice?" said Huntley with hate.

Toward dawn we heard another wheat train approaching. Jess suggested that we position ourselves a couple of hundred yards apart along the track and try to board the train one after another. Smoke hung in the air far off, and the whole train looked tiny, like a single little box. We were tense with excitement.

Huntley was to make the first attempt. He caught hold of one of the cars but was too heavy to follow through with his feet. Hanging by one arm, he twisted around and had to let go, then was thrown into the grass far ahead. As for me, I made no attempt to go along, having completely lost my nerve. Jess had surely boarded a moving train before; he ran along with the train, jumped up and grabbed a handhold, and immediately stood with his feet on the projecting edge of the car.

"The dog, he's going off without us," said Huntley, spitting grass out of his mouth.

Down the track a piece the train suddenly stopped. We saw two train-men overpower Jess and put him off. When Huntley and I ran ahead to see if we could help him, it was too late. The train had already left, and we three vagabonds were back on the prairie together.

Thirst bothered us more and more. For the second time, Huntley had used up his tobacco and had no recourse. Spitting a bit of white saliva into his hand, he demonstrated that he was thirstier than any mortal ever was. So Jess and I shared our tobacco with him for the last time.

Once more we walked and walked toward the west. The day wore on.

A man came toward us on the railroad track, heading east. A vagabond like us, he had a little silk handkerchief around his neck and warmer clothes than we, though his shoes were in bad shape.

"Have you got any food or tobacco?" Huntley asked.

"No, sir," the tramp calmly replied.

We then searched him, checking his pockets and his chest, but he had nothing.

All four of us sat and talked for a while.

"There's nothing for you to do west of here," said the new tramp. "I've been walking two days and nights without finding anybody."

"And what's there for us to do east of here?" Huntley asked. "We've come from that direction, been on the way since early this morning."

But the new tramp induced us to turn around and go east with him. All our trudging since dawn was now wasted, and more than ever we hoped there would come a conductor who would let us board his wheat train.

At first our new companion went at a livelier pace than we, since he weighed less and still had a lot of energy. But toward dark, when we neared the spot where we had slept the previous night, he began to slow down, lagging behind the rest of us.

Jess asked him how long it had been since he had anything to eat, and he answered that it was now the third day.

We kept going for another hour with our weary comrade. When the cold dark closed in on us, we had to lift our feet high, like chickens, to keep from stubbing our boots against the ties. We tried going hand in hand, but Huntley grew lazy and depended on the rest of us to hold him up, so we let go of each other. Finally we lay down to sleep.

IV

At dawn we were again on our feet. It was the same today as yesterday; this time an eastbound wheat train went by without paying any attention to our signals. After that, Huntley clenched his fists and gritted his teeth. He said to the new tramp:

"If you had only had a little tobacco with you, we wouldn't have suffered so much from thirst. What's your name?"

"Fred," the man answered.

"So you're a damn German, aren't you?"

"Yes, by descent."

"I knew it. I could tell by looking at you," said Huntley, hostilely.

Fred had livened up and walked like a champion. He seemed to be sure there was a farm or a little town to the east, but he only talked now and then, without joining in the conversation of us others. In a couple of hours he became tired and lagged behind again. Finally he sat right down, and when we looked back he was still sitting there.

Jess the tramp said: "We must give him some of our food, Noot."

This was mere babble on the part of Jess, who knew I had no food left. He said it to attract our attention to what he was about to do. He went back to Fred and gave him his food.

"You did that just to show off!" I yelled at him in a fit of anger. I could see right through it.

Jess gave a start.

"You don't do anything without wanting to gain our respect," I went on. "That first night, when you stayed awake while we napped, you were careful to see that we knew all about it. You're a fraud. I like Huntley a hundred times as much as you, even though he's a bad character."

"Shut your dirty mouth!" exclaimed Huntley, who did not understand a word of what I had said. "You're jealous of Jess because he's a better human being than you are."

Fred had got what amounted to half of a meal, and it did him a world of good. We started to move on again.

But the food also had a bad effect on Fred. He gradually developed a kind of craziness, going out of his mind. He took to talking more and more, grew bigheaded, pretended to have great plans for a little location on the prairie. There was a wheat train standing on the tracks, he said, and there was a loaded engine that we could set on fire.

"Why would we want to do that?" Huntley asked with some annoyance.

There ensued a ridiculous conversation about this engine.

"When we light it there will be an explosion," Fred explained. "Then people will come running and we can kill them."

"A lot of food that'll provide," Huntley replied scornfully. And he said to me: "This crazy man ought to leave us and go his own way right now. He's a nuisance. We were getting along fine until he came."

After Fred had jabbered for a while, he sank back into his former taciturnity. As we pressed ahead we were all quiet except Huntley, who continued to be talkative.

"What's all this going to amount to?" he said to us around noontime.

"I don't know," I answered.

"No, you don't know. But are you maybe wishing you were back at Orange Flat? And what would you do there?"

"The only thing for us to do is to go straight ahead," said Jess.

In midafternoon we sat and rested for an hour. Huntley commented: "You're not saying anything, Fred."

"You're a baboon," Fred replied, with hatred in his eyes.

This irritated Huntley. "You're so high and mighty that you probably use a shoehorn on those snowshoes there," he said, pointing at Fred's ragged shoes.

Fred only sighed and said nothing. He knew perfectly well that none of us sympathized with him. Later, when we had begun to push on again, Fred would try to get us interested in him by suddenly bending over and picking up a stone or a rusty spike, then examining it very carefully. We others would run over to him, only to be disappointed when we discovered what it was. But Fred succeeded in keeping us interested for a while.

We came upon a dilapidated shack in the middle of the prairie. It had probably stood here since the time the railroad was built. We went in and looked around, but the tramp Fred did not go with us.

Jess and Huntley began to carve their initials in the walls, the way vagrants do, while Fred stayed outside and Huntley went to the door from time to time to keep an eye on him. When he had finished with his initials he went to the door again and looked out.

"There he goes on the run!" Huntley yelled. "The dog, he's running away from us. He must know of a good place to go."

The three of us sprang after the fleeing Fred with a hue and cry as if we were going to take his life. When he saw he was being pursued, he struck out onto the prairie in a great arc, but with the three of us cooperating, there was no way he could escape. Huntley got hold of him, shook him like a child, and demanded to know if he had a good place in mind.

"I don't know of any good place," Fred answered, "but I can't stand being with you guys. You're a bunch of vicious fools. Okay, go ahead, kill me. I don't care."

We put aside our differences and stayed together, continuing on our way until nightfall, when we lay down early on account of exhaustion. Before that, though, I had an altercation with the tramp Jess, who hit me in the face several times because I had called him a fraud.

"That's the ticket, he deserves a beating," said Huntley, watching closely.

At last I caught Jess under the chin with an uppercut and knocked him down. He then let me be.

During the night I heard Jess get up and go out on the prairie, his pant legs scraping against the frost-covered grass. He's up to something, I thought as I quietly followed him in the darkness. After I had gone a few steps, I could hear him get down in the grass and start eating, and I thought I could also smell meat where he was. He still has provisions left! I realized. Silently I went back to where I had been lying and pretended to be asleep. A half hour later Jess also came back and lay down.

Next morning, telling Huntley what I had found out, I insisted that he help me search Jess. Promptly, willingly, Huntley grabbed Jess and held him. It turned out that Jess was carrying bread in three places inside his shirt, bread that was hollowed out and stuffed with meat. This was our salvation. We divided it among all four of us and had a little breakfast. When we had eaten we thanked Jess for the meal and gave him our blessing, even though he had been trying to deceive us. Then Jess, in his shamelessness, began to entertain us, and he whistled like an artist.

We went on. After no more than an hour we could make out some small white squares outlined against the sky ahead of us.

It took us a long time to get near enough to see that it was a farm with wheat fields and irrigation and everything. Before we were quite there, we came upon a woman, a young woman, sitting on a mowing machine and cutting wheat. This was a pleasant sight for us who had been out on the prairie so long and had not seen a woman in a coon's age. She had a big straw hat on her head because of the sun, and she nodded when we said hello to her. Huntley, the first to talk with her, asked her for a little something to eat and drink.

The girl answered that we could have as much as we wanted.

"We took our leave from Orange Flat because the harvest was over with," Huntley said.

Now Jess decided to assert himself and do the right thing, so he said: "No, we ran off from Orange Flat because we weren't getting enough sleep. That's the truth."

"Good!" said the girl.

We all put on airs for her. I held my hat in my hand and talked as politely as I could. Nevertheless, it was our new comrade, Fred the tramp, who won out, because he, the blond German, was the best-looking. She asked him to go home to the farm with her to get victuals, while the rest of us were to take care of her horses. There were no menfolk at home, she said, and she did not dare take all of us with her, lest we frighten her mother.

While Fred and the girl were away, we took turns sitting on the mowing machine and letting the horses go, so that the work would get done, regardless.

In a little while the farm owner appeared. He gathered that we were capable enough, and by the time the young woman came back with the food, her father had engaged all four of us hoboes until the harvesting was over.

V

The harvesting took us five days and the threshing two more, so we got paid for seven days and were free as a bird once again. The tramp Jess quickly made preparations to leave the place—just as he had left a hundred places before—having now ceased to roam for a week. I got ready to join him, but we did not want Huntley or Fred the German with us.

As we stood out in the yard, the farmer said he could use two of us for a month to help with the fall plowing. Huntley was already some distance down the road, and Jess refused to stay any longer, pretending that he had to be back east right away. So Fred and I were picked to remain at the farm.

Jess said to me: "Our agreement was that the two of us would tramp together. At least, come down to the town with me. Now that we have money again, we can look around for a better place than this one here."

So, telling the farmer I would be back tomorrow, I went off with Jess.

After we had walked along the railroad track for a couple of hours, we came to a farm, and after four hours, to another farm. Then we came to the town of Eliot. On the way, Jess had explained to me that a person could discover a lot of little moneymaking opportunities if he did not commit himself forever to some out-of-the-way farm. Now, here was a little town that we could perhaps get to by train.

"I'm going back to the farm tomorrow," I said.

"I know what you've got in your head," said Jess. "It's the girl. You'd better leave her alone. Fred's ahead of you there, has a better chance than you do, owing to his good looks."

"Now, I don't think Fred is such a beauty," I said.

Jess made no response to this, but after a while he remarked: "For that matter, Fred won't get the girl either."

"He won't?" I said, and my heart was glad. "You're damn good at figuring such things out, Jess, and you don't think Fred will get her?"

"The old man won't allow it. What you have to do, if you want to improve your own chances, is to stay away for a time and then come back with a lot of money in your pocket. That's the way."

From now on I burned with the desire to get hold of a lot of money.

We went into a saloon in the town and got something to drink. I was so unused to hard liquor that I soon was filled with joy and laughter. But this did not last long. When a wandering band of musicians came in and began to play the harp and the violin, I quickly felt sad, crying on the inside. I gave some money to the woman with the harp, and Jess gave me a surprised look.

"You're in love. That's a fact," he said.

We moved around from one saloon to another, because we had no other place to go. And we were welcome everywhere, since we came from the West and acted as if we had big money on us. At one of the places we ran into Huntley, who was already quite drunk and came toward us with his pocketknife in his hand, as if he was going to kill us. We refused to associate with him. In the evening we took refuge in the first saloon.

While we stood at the bar, the saloonkeeper carried on a bit of conversation with one of the townspeople, a railroad man who had come in to get a whiskey.

The saloonkeeper said: "I saw Mr. Hart and his wife leave on the train today. Where are they going?"

"To Chicago," the man replied. "He has business there, I hear. His wife is going with him for fun."

"So George will take charge of the bank in the meantime?"

"I suppose so. George is capable enough if he can only stay sober."

This conversation had little interest for me, but my comrade Jess listened closely, then took me outside to talk with me.

We walked slowly through the town, Jess constantly mulling over some idea. We came to a building with a sign that read: "Hart & Co. Farmers Bank." Here Jess told me to wait a minute while he went inside. When he came out I asked him: "What were you doing in there?"

"I changed my last little bill," Jess answered.

We kept walking until we came to the edge of town and sat down near a switch where lumber was stacked beside the rails.

First, Jess went around these piles of lumber to make sure we were alone. Then he came back and said: "Neither of us has any money left, isn't that so?"

"I have a couple of dollars," I replied, looking for them.

"So you have one dollar less than I do. You gave one to that woman with the harp. That was the dumbest thing you could have done."

"Well, it's not much smarter to go to saloons and drink up the money."

"Have you noticed how I drink?" Jess asked. "I drink only a shot when you drink a whole glass. Every time."

"What was it you wanted to talk with me about?" I asked.

"And, besides, I wouldn't have got the plan I have now if we hadn't gone to the saloons," Jess continued.

"What kind of a plan is it?"

"Mr. Hart and Mrs. Hart left for Chicago today," said Jess.

"So what?"

"And George is in charge of the bank for the time being."

"Yeah, so I heard."

"George is Mrs. Hart's brother, according to what I've found out."

"Oh, really?"

"But George is a well-known drunkard."

"I already knew all that, Jess. It doesn't make much sense."

Jess explained himself a little more fully, and I gathered that, in short, he was going to visit the bank tonight or tomorrow night. I was supposed to help him.

"I don't dare," I answered.

"Then I will take Huntley with me."

I didn't like that, either, so I said: "I've never done it before. It sounds so dangerous. But if you will teach me—"

"There's no danger," said Jess. "If George starts to drink, all the rest is easy. I've studied the building."

And Jess showed me a metal saw and a nifty pair of bolt cutters, with jaws like two knives.

"But later?" I said. "Afterward?"

"Afterward we'll be a long way from here," Jess replied. "Mr. Hart needs three days to get to Chicago and three to get back; that's six. He'll be there four days; that's ten altogether." Jess added: "Anyhow, I don't intend to steal all the bank's got. So far as the girl is concerned, what you need is a good nest egg that you can add to by saving."

We wandered around for a couple of hours, during which the stores closed and the street grew lively for a while with people getting off from work. Only the saloons were still open, and they would stay open as long as there were customers.

"Now we must find George and see what he's going to do," said Jess.

And we went from saloon to saloon and drank whiskey and beer, but found George nowhere among the customers. And we took refuge again in that first saloon.

Here we ran into George.

VI

George did not want to join the fun—he said so when he arrived—and for several hours he had steadfastly refrained. It was a nice fall evening, he said later, and it was just as nice over where he was sitting. He sat there for another hour.

He was a fat little man, at least forty years old, with a strangely sensual look. He was well-dressed and had very white hands, since the only work he did was to sit and write. He paid no attention to us.

All at once he began to drink, and to drink a lot. People came in from the street, people he knew, and he turned the evening into a lively party with them. He treated them all with great courtesy. But when Jess went to the bar and asked him to drink with him, George brushed him off, being a big man in the town while Jess was nothing but a tramp.

"Go ahead, drink with him," said the saloonkeeper. "The two gentlemen have plenty of money," he added, referring to Jess and me.

"That's more than I have," George responded, and he showed his wallet, which contained several bills.

From now on he took responsibility for all expenses, treating everyone who wanted a drink. The saloonkeeper did his best to satisfy him.

"I've got to get some more money," George said. "Wait for me here, boys." Out he went, in the best of humor, singing.

"A wonderful guy!" the boys said to one another. "He'll keep it up all night!"

Jess was listening to every word.

When George came back he pretended at first that he had not found any more money, but he unconcernedly ordered one round of drinks after another and paid lavishly with bills from his wallet. This went on for a couple of hours.

"Now we're going over to Conway's," George announced. Conway's was another saloon.

"He's closed," said the saloonkeeper.

"Then we'll break in," said George. "Come on, boys."

Jess and I held back, as if we were proud.

"Won't you two come along?" George asked. "I'm inviting you."

And we let ourselves be persuaded.

Conway's was not closed. There was also a happy company gathered there, and George and his boys were welcomed. As for us, Jess no longer wanted to keep so quiet, but began to whistle like an artist, provoking great applause.

"He's damn good at whistling!" they all said.

Our group stayed there two hours and drank huge quantities of liquor. I sipped shots the whole time, as Jess had taught me, and they had little effect on me, since I was under such tension because of what lay ahead.

After counting his bills, George said: "Now I'm going to the girls. Good night, boys. I must go after more money."

"You still have a lot of money," someone objected.

"Not enough," George answered, and he staggered out the door.

"The bank will be several hundred dollars poorer after tonight," said the boys.

"It looks that way," Jess promptly agreed. "He's an expert at spending money."

But none of them would talk to Jess, he being a tramp, and they all drew away from us.

Jess went over to the bar and asked each one individually what he would like to drink, but all of them said no thanks, they did not want any more.

"Come, have a whiskey," he said to me.

I looked at him in wonderment.

"You need it," said Jess.

And I drank two big glasses of whiskey, which made me feel so strong and invincible that I could have started throwing people out of Conway's.

Jess and I said good-night and went out to the street. The town was dark and deserted. With Jess directing, we headed for the bank. There were lights in the windows, so we knew George must be inside.

"Wait here!" said Jess, and he made five soundless leaps toward the building, then disappeared through the yard gate.

Where could he have gone? I wondered.

I had waited two minutes when Jess came back. He made the same leaps.

"Where have you been?" I asked.

"I've been at the door and fiddled a bit with the lock," Jess replied. "Let's just wait here a while."

Suddenly Jess grabbed me by the arm and whispered: "Do you hear that?"

We could hear a man working and working with his key in the lock while swearing more and more freely.

"That's George," said Jess.

We hid behind a corner of the building and waited.

"I can't get the damn door to lock again," said George as he came out to the street. "Oh, well, there are two locks on the safe."

George proceeded toward the girls, staggering badly.

"Now we'll take a little tour until everything is quiet," said Jess.

While we were walking I said: "I still don't think you dare do it, Jess."

"Just wait!" said Jess.

Looking at the buildings as closely as he could in the dark, he picked out a shop with double doors and said he would show me something. Staggering as if helpless, he threw himself with full force against the doors. The whole building shook and both doors sprang open.

From inside the shop a watchman called out: "What the hell is that?"

Jess just stood there swaying in the doorway as if he did not know, himself, how he had come to be there.

"Who's there?" demanded the man in the shop. "I'll shoot you, you son of a bitch, if you don't answer."

"It's me," said Jess as if dead drunk, and he let himself sink down on the floor.

So, on top of everything, the man in the shop had to drag him out to the sidewalk. And Jess weaved about, the way drunks do, so convincingly that the watchman clearly assumed this had been an involuntary break-in. But he was furious as he shut and locked the doors again.

"Too bad there was a man in the shop," Jess said when he came up to me on the street. "Otherwise, I would have made a little haul."

"I realize now that you have the guts for absolutely anything," I said.

We were standing near the bank once again. Jess said: "You gather up a fistful of sand here on the street and throw it at the windows if anybody comes."

"Okay," I said. I could hear my heart beating.

"I'm going now," said Jess.

I watched him until he disappeared inside the yard gate. If someone were to come along now and ask me why I was standing here, what could I say? I gathered up a handful of sand and got rid of the pebbles in it. The street, unpaved, was full of dry sand in the wagon tracks. There was no traffic, nothing to be seen. The town was quiet except for an occasional whistle down at the depot where locomotives were switching wheat cars. Suddenly I heard steps on the plank sidewalk. I was about to throw sand at the bank's windowpanes but, instead, went up to the approaching pedestrian, said "Good evening," and got a reply in kind. And the man went on his way. By now, Jess must have been gone for five minutes.

I began to hear, quite distinctly, little clicking sounds, one after another, coming from inside the bank building. Jess is cutting bolts, I thought, amazed at his cold-bloodedness. I knew where I would run in case of necessity—down to the railroad, to the many sheds and storage places along the tracks.

It was taking a long time, an eternity. As Jess began to saw metal in there, I could barely hear a few of the strokes, and I was on pins and needles on account of the risk he was willing to take. "If only he can manage to steal a decent amount!" I thought, greedy for my share. As time passed, I calmed down and started walking back and forth on the sidewalk and thinking. I was thinking of the girl on the farm. Alice Rodgers was her name.

By now, Jess had surely been away for at least an hour, and he was not back yet. I had just begun to get up enough nerve to go into the yard and peek in the windows—when Jess came out. He hurried ahead of me down to the lumber piles by the railroad tracks.

"Goddamn this bad luck!" he said, catching his breath after having worked so hard.

"What's the matter?" I asked.

"That damn George must have taken the whole bank with him to the girls," said Jess. "The safe was empty. There was nothing in it but bank records."

At this report, a feeling of satisfaction ran through me, and I gave myself away to Jess when I cheerfully patted him on the shoulder and asked: "So, did you take anything?"

"What should I have taken, you stupid ass?" Jess angrily replied. "I'm not going to sit here any longer," he added, further showing his irritation. "We must try something else."

With that, Jess set out, following the rails down to the station, and I went along with him.

I was feeling relaxed after my long vigil. I said: "To tell the truth, I don't think there's any use trying anything else, either. Let's give it up."

"Let's try just one more thing," said Jess.

He went into the station and asked the telegrapher what time the next eastbound train was due. "In half an hour," the telegrapher answered, glancing at the clock.

"There's nothing for us to do until after the train has come and gone," Jess said to me.

Though we were freezing, we sat outside the station and waited the half hour. It was nearly morning.

As soon as we heard the train coming, Jess got up and told me to wait for him where I was. He went back into the station and stayed.

I waited. The train came and went. I sat there waiting for an hour longer, while dawn began to appear in the east. I thought Jess was probably out reconnoitering. Finally I went into the station and asked the man whether he had seen my comrade.

"He left on the train," the telegrapher answered.

"Oh, he left on the train," I said, trying not to show my surprise. I had begun to be suspicious of Jess, wondering whether he might have found something besides records in the bank. He had become so agitated and behaved so strangely toward me.

Smiling, the telegrapher asked: "Did he run off from you?"

I gave him a supercilious smile in return and answered that No, I knew he was leaving.

"He was no friend of mine," I said, "and I told him just now that I wouldn't have anything to do with him."

I went out of the station with a thousand thoughts. I was flabbergasted by Jess's nerve. Of course, his luck had held up, the scoundrel, and he had found oodles of money in the bank. And he hadn't remembered me with the least bit of it. To hell with him!

During the day I had noticed the sign of a rooming house, and I now started up the street to get a bed there. On the way I became more and more self-satisfied for not having dirtied my hands with the stolen money. What a pleasure it is to live a marvelously pure and undefiled life in this world! I reflected, trembling with joy. Let me remain poor, let me slave for others, to the last drop of my blood!

When I arrived at the rooming house, I decided I would rather go down to the lumber piles and sleep gratis. I had only two dollars left, and I wanted to be able to take home for Alice Rodgers a gilded penholder that I had seen in a jeweler's window.

VII

"I was thinking you had gone down east with your friend," said the farmer Rodgers when I got back to the farm. "I like the way you keep your word."

"Yes, indeed, I said I would come back today," I answered. "As for my friend, he was no friend when we parted. I refused to go along with him."

"It's going to be cold for you to sit on the plow with those shoes on," Mr. Rodgers said. "You should have bought a new pair when you were in town and had the money."

I was sent out on the prairie to pick, myself, the team of mules I wanted. I started the whole herd running, watched to see which animals would look for each other like a couple, and then made my choice accordingly.

"That's my team," said Alice when I brought them in to be harnessed. "Be nice to them!"

"I sure will, Miss," I answered. I added that "Miss" as if she were a lady. Ordinarily, we did not use it on the farm.

I did not get to keep Alice's team very long. One day a mule of Fred the German's team fell over and died of an intestinal obstruction. Fred then proposed to take over my team. I objected to this, and old Rodgers himself was on my side, but Alice and Fred won out over us. Next morning Fred got up earlier than usual, and when I went to the barn my team was gone. This was good enough grounds for me to leave the farm, but Mr. Rodgers said I should not let it bother me; I should just go and pick another team. I found myself a new team that was at least as good as the previous one and, in fact, had more endurance. Taking good care of my animals—feeding them well, currying them and washing their hooves regularly—I was soon able to leave Fred quite a ways behind me in the plowing.

During the first week on the farm, I worried a lot for fear the scoundrel Jess's break-in would be discovered and I would be involved in his crime. But when the town of Eliot's two little weeklies arrived at the farm, there was nothing in either of them about the break-in. So, recovering my composure, I stopped worrying about the subject. Either Jess had not broken into the safe after all, but was only trying to impress me with his daring, or the bank was robbed, all right, but George, for his own sake, did not dare report it. I heard later that George was the son of a wealthy millowner, so the father may well have made good the deficit.

Every day Fred beat my time with Alice. No matter what I did, he stood in my way and won out. During the harvest he had already begun to pretty himself up more than the rest of us, and before going in for meals he would stand a long time combing and parting his light hair. It bothered him that, when he laughed, the gap was visible where he had lost one of his eyeteeth. But what could I say—I who had lost almost all my hair on the prairie and had been practically bald for a year! Besides, I had stopped shaving and let my beard grow, to be streaked by sun and weather, as my eyebrows also were. I could not compare with Fred.

However, old Rodgers and his wife were very friendly toward me and treated me well. At the table Mrs. Rodgers would often tell me that I must eat more pudding or cookies. Now and then she asked me, with great interest, what things were like in the country I was from, but she never asked Fred, since he was born in America, right here in Dakota, in the town of Fargo.

One morning Alice was all dressed up. I thought she must be going to town, and I did all I could to get to drive her there, but it turned out that she was dressed up merely because it was Sunday. I went to work as usual and thought no more about the matter, but in a little while I saw Alice in all her finery go over to Fred far out on the prairie and pay him a visit. She did not come to me.

So it went every day. I made no progress with Alice, though I called her "Miss" and was very attentive. Fred was more natural than I, never putting himself out in the least. I began to think I was making too much effort. But I had already spoiled Alice, and when I stopped saying "Miss" and simply called her Alice, she took it as rudeness on my part and would not answer me.

One day I tried a trick that I had thought up. There was a thunderstorm that lasted several hours, so it was impossible to plow, and we unhitched our teams and went home. I had no dry jacket but did have a dry shirt, and putting it on I sat with the family in the living room where it was warm. To show my beautiful penmanship, I began to write a couple of letters, writing with the gilded penholder and pretending to be used to it.

"I've never seen his like as a writer!" said Mrs. Rodgers in amazement. Alice cast an unwilling glance at me. She spoke not to me but to Fred, who also was sitting there.

"Do you use a gold penholder?" she said.

I asked: "Do you think it's pretty?"

"Yes."

"You're welcome to it," I said, handing it to her.

"I? I don't want it," she responded, curtly. "But I'm surprised that you'd be using such an expensive penholder."

"One uses what one has," I said. I went on to intimate that a girl had given it to me. But this made no impression on her either. Despite my trick, I could not get her to accept the penholder.

I kept trying my best, laying one plan after another, to win her over. One week I experimented with being silent and reserved in the hope that she would feel a feminine sympathy for me. Another week I was full of fun and tried to shine with my repartee. Alice merely said:

"How long have you been in America?"

"Over six years altogether," I replied. "I'm here now for the second time."

"And you, Freddie?"

"I was born here," answered Fred.

"You see the difference," said Alice to me.

For it was finest to be born an American. That's why she called him Freddie instead of Fred—so that he would be American rather than German.

"Look at his hair!" said Alice, referring to Fred's. "It's like gold. What have you done with your hair, Noot?"

"I lost it on the prairie," I said. "But now I think it's beginning to take root again and will be coming back."

"Oh, yeah?" said Alice.

VIII

A day was to come when my star would rise high, and for a short time I would be the conquering lord of the farm. Those were proud hours.

The Rodgers's young grandson, Edwin, was visiting them. The little fellow spent much of the time with me, accompanying me out on the prairie, where I took him up on the plow and let him drive the team. One day, when he was at home on the farm with his grandfather, he was hurt in an accident. The old man was occupied with sending some planks down the steps from the loft of an outbuilding when one of the planks slid off to one side. A corner of the plank struck the child above the ear, and he fell over and lay as if dead.

There was great weeping and wailing in the yard. Alice called to me, who was nearest, to come home at once. I tore the mules loose from the plow, letting them go wherever they wanted, and ran home. No doubt Alice had turned to me unintentionally. On second thought, she also called Fred, because she trusted him more. At her urging, Fred hastily hitched the team of horses to the wagon and hurried to town for a doctor.

When I got home the grandparents were desperate, unable to control their bawling. Mr. Rodgers rolled the child back and forth on the living-room floor without getting him to show any sign of life. An old memory from childhood came to my assistance, and I knew at once what I had to do. "Take off his jacket," I said. I ran to get my razor, which was under the pillow on my bed. When I came back I pulled up Edwin's shirtsleeve and began to cut into a vein in his arm.

The women gave a shriek and threw themselves upon me as if crazy. Alice, in particular, was unreasonable, accusing me of trying to kill the child. I stomped on the floor and ordered her away. This was a matter of life or death, and I was going to save the child! Old Rodgers, yielding at these strong words, helped me hold the child's arm. He only asked: "Will bleeding do any good?"

When I had cut deep enough, blood began to come, at first in little drops, later in a fine stream. I opened Edwin's shirt and listened to his chest; his heart was not beating. Then I took him by the legs and swung him back and forth with his head down, whereupon the blood began to flow. I laid him down and listened again—his heart was beating a little. This was the nicest thing I could wish for. We all stood there looking at the child. The tiny fingers on one hand moved a bit. "There, he moved his fingers!" said Mr. Rodgers, almost suffocated with joy. "He moved his fingers!" the old grandmother repeated and went sobbing out of the room. A little later the child opened a pair of bewildered eyes and closed them again. "He looked up!" said Mr. Rodgers. "He's alive." Calling his wife back in, he said the same thing to her.

"Fetch me a soft cloth," I said to Alice.

Alice was away a long time. Meanwhile, growing impatient and masterful, I grabbed the first thing I caught sight of—a piece of white linen that was being made into something. I tore out a square of it for a dressing and ripped off a long strip for a bandage.

When Alice came back she said: "Have you torn my pretty bonnet to pieces?"

"I'll pay you for it," I answered, still picking at the cloth to shred it.

Mrs. Rodgers, completely done in by my masterful performance, said to her daughter: "Be still, Alice."

Edwin opened his eyes again and again, whimpering. Soon he tried to reach up to his head and feel his wound, which I kept him from doing. Then he looked up with a steady gaze, and I could tell that he recognized me.

I now lay the dressing on the opened vein and tied the bandage around his arm, which I could hardly have done before. We carried him to his bed and undressed him. While he dozed off, I washed the wound on his head and tied a bandage around it too.

"Now let the doctor come!" I said. And I felt like a god.

Once the tension was over, I came undone and started to collapse. I sank down on a chair. In a little while I got up and went out of the house with my knees shaking. I sat down behind the barn and blacked out. I must have sat there for ten minutes. Then, coming to, I went out after my mules, hitched them up, and began to plow again. I could have slept on the seat.

After I had been plowing for two or three hours, old Mr. Rodgers came out to me to say the doctor had been there, rebandaged Edwin's wound, and given him some drops. Mr. Rodgers told me to quit for the day.

I unhitched the mules and went home with him. Hardly a word was said between us, but I could see how grateful the old man was.

Old Mrs. Rodgers came to meet us and said to me: "The doctor has been here. He's sure Edwin will make it."

"He said you had done the right thing in bleeding him," Rodgers said.

"He said you saved his life," the wife added.

And again I felt like a proud lord and master.

For the rest of the day I wandered around doing nothing. But it was no fun having nothing to do, and I was bored as I went from one place to another on the farm. Had it not been for my pride, I would have got back on the plow. Alice could have lowered herself enough to say a few encouraging words to me. Instead, she came up to me and said bitterly:

"You stomped on the floor at me, Noot. You must never do that again."

She seemed so impossible that I could not bring myself to say a single word in response. But the old folks got it into their heads that I was certainly a remarkable man, an expert of great versatility. They listened attentively to everything I said, and both of them seemingly began to make a little distinction between Fred and me—in my favor. Thus one day I was sent to town to deliver wheat and do some shopping, and he did not go along.

But even if I had been a wizard, I could not have made do forever with only one miracle. As the days went by and little Edwin recovered, everything became just as it was before. My great accomplishment was pretty much forgotten, and again I felt miserable and defeated as I went about the farm. Nothing had changed.

Fred came up to me and said: "The frost will be here soon and the plowing will be over. What are you going to do then?"

"I don't really know," I answered. "But something will probably turn up."

Fred and I got along well together, with no antagonism between us. I did not blame him for taking my team. That was Alice's fault. By no means a bad tramp, Fred had become unemployed and taken up the vagrant life for the first time this year. He was vain about his pretty face, though, and when he laughed he barely opened his mouth, because he wanted to hide the gap where he had lost a tooth. It made him look as if he had a crack in his lip. Still, it became him to open his mouth so sparingly, since he had rather thick lips naturally. "Laugh some more!" Alice would say to him. She was head over heels in love.

Though I was worse off, my love being unrequited, Fred did not have it too good. He told me that Alice had spoken to her parents about him, had told them she loved him, but they insisted that she give him up.

Fred said to me: "You must help us, Noot."

I felt myself honored a bit by this request, and I asked: "Did Alice want you to ask me?"

"Yes," said Fred, "it was her idea."

I said: "Then I'll do it."

It crossed my mind that, with my incredible magnanimity, I might be able to cut Fred out.

Having the ear of the two old folks, I asked Mrs. Rodgers one day whether she came from a farm or from a town.

"From a farm," Mrs. Rodgers answered.

"It must be strange for a young girl on a lonely farm," I went on. "How does anyone meet people?"

Mrs. Rodgers answered that there were farms all around now. And there was the weekly trip to town. But, of course, there really were not many opportunities to meet people.

"And how does a person get married?" I asked. "Do they simply take someone who happens to pass by?"

At this, the two old folks looked at one another. They had an older daughter who ran off with a man who happened to pass by. But things had turned out well for this young couple, who had taken up land and become farmers. Little Edwin was their son.

"It must be chancy," I persisted. "A young girl could easily fall in love with an unworthy man just because she didn't know anyone else and had no choice."

Yes, I was absolutely right about that. It often happened.

"A person certainly ought to be careful about people like us who come along on foot," I said finally.

The two old folks looked at one another again. They understood me to a tee.

The old mother will tell this to her daughter! I thought. For the time being, Alice will probably not give Fred up, but she will get an inkling of the unhappy prospect that I foresee!

Before long I myself became fearful on account of what I had said. I had gone too far, and Alice would undoubtedly realize that I had worked against Fred. So I took the first opportunity to tell Mrs. Rodgers that with Fred it was another matter, that he was without any question a fine man, a veritable gem, one that I would choose if I were a girl. This time, too, I got the old woman to listen to me, and I noticed that it dawned on her what an unselfish soul I was.

One evening, just as it was getting dark, I ran into Alice and let her speak first.

"You're no friend of Freddie's," she said.

"Why, what have I done?"

"You've done him a bad turn."

I took Alice with me in to her mother and asked whether I had said anything bad about Fred.

"You said we should be leery of tramps, but Fred was an exception and a gem," the mother replied.

"But, mother, you didn't tell me that!" cried Alice. "God bless you, Noot."

I went off proud and offended, making the most of the advantage I had gained. The next time Fred asked me for help, I told him that, because of the way Alice had acted, I would have nothing more to do with his affair.

IX

Alice approached me, weeping, and asked me to speak to her parents again in Fred's behalf. This was in the evening after the day's work was all done. Alice came right up to me, closer than she had ever been before, so close I could feel her breath, and began to pick at my shirt buttons. Thrilled by my good luck, I replied incoherently: "About Fred? Well. What shall I say? I'll do anything you want."

I did not know that Fred was eavesdropping, but he was standing in the barn listening to us.

"What should I do, anyway?" I asked. "Do you know what you're expecting of me? You surely realize that I'm in love with you myself."

"No, I didn't realize it," she answered. "You never told me."

"No, I've never told you. I keep my feet on the ground. I know I'm just a tramp. I'm not good enough for you."

"Well, that's neither here nor there," said Alice. "It's Freddie I love."

"And you ask me for help!"

"No, no," she said. "Let it go, then."

"Has it never occurred to you that I've already been quite unselfish?" I said. "I've not heard a word of thanks from you. It's not humanly possible for me to go any farther."

"I know you're a good person," said Alice.

"Is that all?"

"I also know you're a learned man, one who knows a lot about everything. You write like a flash."

But Alice did not say what I wanted to hear—that I was almost as good-looking and almost as charming as Fred.

"Couldn't you ever learn to care for me?" I asked.

"Well, yes," said Alice, "a little. That is—"

Trying to ingratiate myself further, I asked: "Don't you think I could run our farm and make good money and support you well? But what can Fred do?"

Alice was silent.

"You don't know what kind of a man I am," I said, mysteriously, and suggested that she did not have the slightest conception of me.

"But I have!" exclaimed Fred, suddenly emerging from the barn. He had a pitchfork in his hands and was raging. "I know what kind of a man you are! You're evil, nothing but a scoundrel, and I'm going to kill you like a dog."

Frightened, I lifted my arm to defend myself. "Calm down, Fred," I pleaded. "Let me go."

"Go? I'm going to kill you right now!" Fred yelled, jabbing the pitchfork at me.

Alice showed no sign of interceding. She merely said: "Don't kill him."

"You're a murderer," I said to Fred. "I'm begging you to put down that pitchfork, you murderer."

But Fred was not about to spare me. He said: "If you move an inch, I'll run you through."

I sat down on the ground. Fred, I saw, was so raving mad that I could not do a thing with him. It was common knowledge that a pitchfork stab was slow to heal—might never heal—and I feared for my life.

"What did you tell the old folks about me?" Fred screamed.

"You're a stupid ass," I said. "I haven't told them anything, and I'm not going to do you any favors."

Fred turned the pitchfork around and hit me in the head with the handle. It did not hurt very much. I got back up. The next time the pitchfork came near me I grabbed it away. Alice, realizing that Fred was now in danger, ran into the house and brought her father out.

"Take it easy, boys," said Mr. Rodgers. "What's going on?"

"Ask Fred," I replied. "He came running with a pitchfork."

"They took turns with the pitchfork," said Alice.

I now realized that Alice was a sorry specimen of a human being, and though I was a sorry one myself, she was much worse. Angrily I went my way and left the two lovers to make whatever explanations and excuses they wanted to behind my back. The next day I went over to where Fred was plowing and ordered him to step down off the plow. He refused. I then gave him a punch in the jaw that staggered him and caused him to fall off the seat. Fred found no other way to get revenge than to cut the back of my jacket to shreds one night while I was asleep.

We kept plowing until ice formed on the fields, indeed, until it began to freeze deep down in the ground. One day Mr. Rodgers said: "Now, boys, the plowing must stop."

We quickly unhitched and headed for home. And for the last time I curried my mules, washed their hooves, and gave them something to eat.

"It's getting dark, it'll soon be night," said Mr. Rodgers. "You can stay till tomorrow."

He figured out what we were owed and paid us the money. I had not taken anything in advance, so I got more than Fred, who had received advances for new clothes and a new hat from town.

Mr. Rodgers offered to lend me, for my trip, a jacket that was somewhat better than mine. He said I could leave it with his wheat dealer. I turned the jacket pockets inside out to show that nothing had been left in them. This was an unnecessary little trick of mine to demonstrate my honesty.

That night I woke up to find Fred getting out of his bunk and putting on his jacket.

"Where are you going?" I asked. He did not answer.

Fred went out and stayed out. He's up to something! I thought, sneaking to the door and opening it. It was dark and cold outside, with few stars in the sky. I did not feel like following him and spying on him, but went back in, chilled to the bone. Whatever was going on, it was best for me to keep out of it. I fell sound asleep and did not wake up until morning.

Fred had not come back by the time I got up and went into the house to join the old folks.

"Where's Fred?" asked Mrs. Rodgers, who had breakfast ready.

"I don't know," I answered.

She went out and called him, but there was no response. Then, getting suspicious, the old woman went to Alice's room, threw open the door, and looked in. The room was empty. Closing the door, she said: "Where in the world is Alice?" Her face was ashen.

We looked high and low for the two of them, without success. But Alice's team was gone from the barn, so we realized that the pair had run off.

"Just like our oldest daughter," said Mrs. Rodgers, bewildered.

Old man Rodgers fretted but kept still. He went around doing one thing and another, without keeping at anything. His wife, the first to come to her senses, said it had gone well for their other daughter and maybe it would be okay with this one too. So far as the grandparents were concerned, it was no longer their grown children who were dearest to them, but their little grandchildren. Little Edwin was the greatest joy of their home.

"If you come past here again, I'll sure give you work if I have any," Mr. Rodgers said to me. "Where are you traveling to?"

"Farther west," I answered.

"You shouldn't do that," said Rodgers. "You ought to get yourself a place down here in town and stay in this part of the country."

But I made my way to the vineyards of California.

A Woman's Victory

Though not published until 1905, nearly twenty years after Hamsun's service as a streetcar conductor, this story may have originated in his fantasizing while on the job. Such fantasizing could help to account for his reputation as an absent-minded employee. Hamsun implies that he worked for the streetcar company longer than he actually did. By the 1887 Christmas season, the time he gives for the events in the main part of the story, he was no longer in Chicago but had returned to Minneapolis.

I was a streetcar conductor in Chicago.

At first I was assigned to the Halsted line, which was a horse tramway running from the center of the city clear down to the Stockyards. Those of us who had night duty on this line did not feel particularly safe, what with all the rough-looking passengers we got at night. We were not allowed to shoot and kill people, because of the damages that the streetcar company would have to pay. As for me, I didn't even own a gun, so I had to depend on luck. Still, one is seldom completely weaponless. On the brake there was a crank that could be quickly taken off and used to great effect. Actually, I did not have to use it more than once.

During the Christmas season, 1886, I served on my streetcar night after night without anything happening. Then, from the Stockyards, came a big bunch of Irishmen who completely filled the car. Drunk, carrying their bottles with them, they were unwilling to pay, even though we had already begun to move. They said they had paid the company five cents every morning and evening for a whole year, and now that it was Christmas they were not going to pay. Their attitude was reasonable enough, but I could not let them ride free, for fear of company "spies" who checked up on us conductors. A policeman got on the car, stood there a few minutes, said something about Christmas and the weather, then jumped off, the car being so crowded. I knew perfectly well that, at a word from me to the policeman, all the passengers would have had to pay their nickel, but I kept quiet. "Why didn't you report us?" one of them asked. I answered that I did not think I needed to, for I had gentlemen to deal with. At this, some began to laugh uproariously, but two came to my support and made it possible for me to collect from all of them.

The next Christmas I was on the Cottage line, which was quite different. I now had a train of two and sometimes three cars, and it was propelled by an underground cable. The population in this part of the city was so refined that I had to wear gloves when collecting my nickels. There was no tension here, and it soon became boring to look at these suburbanites and listen to them.

Something rather interesting happened, though, during that Christmas season of 1887.

On the day before Christmas, in the morning, I was going down to the city with my train; I was then on daytime duty. A gentleman stepped aboard and engaged me in conversation. When I had to go through the cars he waited until I came back to my place on the rearmost platform. Then he began to talk again. He was about thirty years old, pale, with a mustache, very well-dressed but without an overcoat, though it was fairly cold.

"I dashed off from home just as I was," he explained. "I wanted to get ahead of my wife."

"The Christmas present," I suggested.

"Right!" he answered with a smile. But it was a strange smile, a grimace, a mocking grin.

"How much do you make?" he asked.

That is not an unusual question in Yankeeland, and I told him what my wages were.

"Would you like to earn ten dollars extra?" he asked.

I answered: "Yes."

Without further ado, he took out his pocketbook and handed me a ten-dollar bill. He said he trusted me.

"What am I supposed to do? " I asked.

After requesting to see my schedule, he said: "You have eight hours to-day?"

"Yes."

"On one of your trips you are to do me a favor. Here at the corner of Monroe Street the train passes over a pit that gives access to the underground cable. On top of the pit is a lid that I will lift off and then step down into the hole."

"You're going to commit suicide?"

"Not quite. But I'll pretend to."

"Ah."

"You are to stop your train and get me up out of the hole, even though I resist."

"That I will do."

"Thanks. Now, I'm not crazy, as you perhaps think. I'm doing all this for the sake of my wife, so she can see that I wanted to die."

"Your wife will be on that same train?"

"Yes. She will be sitting in the grip."

I was taken aback. The grip was the driver's car, the one where he stood and controlled the train. It was open, without sides, and no one rode there on a cold winter day.

"She will be riding on the grip," the man repeated. "She has promised in a letter to her lover to ride there today and give him a signal that she is coming. I have read the letter."

"Okay. But I must caution you to be quick about taking the lid off the pit and stepping down in the hole. Otherwise, another train may overtake us. We run at three-minute intervals."

"I know all that," the man replied. "The lid will be loosened when I get there. In fact, it's loose already, this very moment."

"One more thing. How can you tell which train your wife will be on?"

"I will get a telephone call. I have people watching my wife's every step. And she will be wearing a brown fur coat. You can easily recognize her; she is very pretty. If she should faint, carry her into the drugstore on the corner of Monroe."

I asked: "Have you also talked with my driver?"

"Yes," said the man. "And I have paid the driver the same as you. But I don't want you two to discuss the matter. You are not to mention it to each other."

"No."

"When you approach Monroe Street, you are to stand on the grip and carefully keep watch. When you see my head above the pit, give the order to stop, and the train will come to a halt. The driver will help you to over-power me and drag me up out of the hole, despite my insistence that I want to die."

After thinking about the whole thing a bit, I said: "It occurs to me that you could have saved yourself some money and not involved anyone else in your project. You could have just climbed down into the hole."

"But my God!" the man burst out. "What if the driver didn't notice me! What if you didn't notice me! Nobody!"

"You're right."

We continued to talk about one thing and another. The man stayed on the car until the very end of the line, and when my train turned around he accompanied me on the way back.

At the corner of Monroe Street he said: "There is the drugstore where you will take my wife if she faints."

Then he jumped off.

I was ten dollars richer. Thank God, life still had its lucky days! On ac-count of the bitter wind, I had gone all winter with a layer of newspapers over my chest and back. With every movement I crackled in an embar-rassing way, and my fellow workers made a lot of fun of me. Now I would be able to afford a wonderfully impervious leather vest. The next time one of my comrades poked me just to hear me crackle, I would not have to put up with it.

I made two, then three trips downtown, and nothing happened. When I was about to start out from the Cottage station for the fourth time, a young woman stepped aboard and took a seat on the grip. She had on a brown fur coat. When I went up to her and took her fare, she looked me straight in the face. She was young and extremely pretty, with blue, utter-ly innocent eyes.

You poor thing, I thought, you will probably get a terrible fright today, but you have no doubt done something naughty, and now you will be pun-ished for it. Anyhow, it will be a pleasure for me to carry you gently into the drugstore.

We rolled along toward the city. From my platform I observed the driv-er suddenly beginning to talk with the woman. What could he possibly have to say to her? No matter, he was not allowed to chat with passengers while on duty. To my great amazement, I saw the woman move to a seat close to where the driver stood and listen intently to what he was saying.

We rolled farther in toward downtown, stopped and took people on, stopped and let people off, all of them minding their own business. We were approaching Monroe Street. I thought this eccentric young man had made a smart choice for his site. Monroe was a relatively quiet corner where he was not likely to be interfered with when he climbed down into the pit. And I remembered having seen the streetcar company's men stand in these pits to fix whatever went wrong down there. But if a man were to keep standing in the hole when a train went by, he would quickly become several inches shorter, for the claw that reached from the grip down to the cable would tear his head off.

When Monroe was the next street, I went forward to the grip.

Neither the driver nor the woman was talking anymore. I saw the driver nod as if he agreed with something, then stare straight ahead and drive on at full speed. As usual, big Pat the Irishman was my driver.

"Slack her a bit!" I told him. That was the customary jargon, meaning: Drive a little slower. In front of us, in the middle of the tracks, I could make out a black spot that might be a human head protruding from the ground.

I looked at the woman. She had her eyes fixed on the same spot and was holding tightly onto the seat. Already worried about a possible accident! I thought. What will she do when she sees that it is her own husband who wants to die!

But big Pat did not slow down. I yelled to him that there was somebody in the pit—to no effect. By now, we could clearly see the head; it belonged to the rash young man, who was standing in the hole with his face turned toward us. I put my whistle in my mouth and blew as hard as I could, thus giving the signal to stop. Pat kept going at the same speed. In a few seconds there would be a disaster. I rang the warning bell, then leapt forward and grabbed the brake. But it was too late. The train went across the pit before it screeched to a halt.

I jumped off. Bewildered, I could only remember that I was supposed to take hold of a man, who would offer resistance. I immediately got back up on the grip and bustled aimlessly about. The driver also appeared to be dazed. Senselessly, he asked whether there had been someone in the pit, and how it happened that the train had not stopped. The young woman cried: "Terrible! Terrible!" Her face was bloodless, and she sat as if paralyzed. But she did not faint, and after a while she stepped down from the grip and went her way.

A crowd gathered. We found the victim's head under the last car, his body still standing in the pit. The machine's claw had caught him under the chin and taken his head off.

We got the remains out of the tracks, and a policeman came to take them away. The policeman wrote down quite a few names, and all the passengers could testify that I had blown the whistle, rung the bell, and finally grabbed the brake. We streetcar employees ourselves had to submit reports to our office.

Big Pat asked me for my knife. Misunderstanding his purpose, I told him that enough tragedy had already occurred. He smiled and, showing me his revolver, assured me that he was not going to use the knife for any foolishness but had something quite different in mind. As he took the knife he told me goodbye and said he could no longer keep the job, because it bothered him too much. He added that I would have to drive the train to the terminal, where I could get another driver. He explained how I should manage. As for the knife, I could leave it with him, he said. He would use it to cut the buttons off his uniform as soon as he could do so without being seen.

With that, he left me.

There was nothing I could do except drive the train to the terminal myself. Several trains were lined up behind me waiting for me to get out of the way. And since I already had a little practice with the machine, it ran along smoothly enough.

One evening between Christmas and New Year's I was wandering around the city during my time off. When I came to a railroad station, I went inside to watch the hectic traffic. I walked out on one of the platforms, where I looked at a train that was about to leave. All at once I heard my name—on the steps of one of the coaches a man was standing, smiling, and calling to me. It was big Pat. It took a little while for me to recognize him, for he was well-dressed and had shaved off his beard.

I called back to him.

"Sh, not so loud!" Pat said, then asked: "Really, how did it go with the affair?"

"We've been interrogated," I answered. "They're looking for you."

Pat said: "I am traveling to the West. Think what it's like out there. Seven, eight dollars a week, and four of it can be saved. I'll get land, I'll be a farmer. I have money with me, of course. If you'll come along we can find us a fruit farm somewhere out near Frisco."

"I can't go," I replied.

"While I think of it, here is your knife. Thanks for lending it. You see, there's no future in the streetcar life. I worked at it for three years and never got a chance to break away until now."

The locomotive whistled.

"Well, goodbye," said Pat. "Listen, how much did you get from the man we ran over?"

"Ten dollars."

"So did I. Considering everything, he paid quite well. But his wife paid better."

"His wife?"

"Yes, the young woman. I made a little deal with her. And she didn't mind going up to a thousand or two, since she wanted to get rid of her husband. It's due to her money that I can now begin an easier life."

MELLOW REMINISCENCE
(1928, 1949)

Festina Lente

This essay, which appeared in Aftenposten, *December 12, 1928, was more flat-tering than most of what Hamsun had previously written about the United States, but it repeated his familiar complaint about American materialism. Fes-tina lente (make haste slowly), he advised Americans. Despite his criticism of the modern and mechanical, he used the latest machinery, including a Fordson trac-tor, as a gentleman farmer on his Nørholm estate. His objection to American iso-lationism makes him sound almost like a League of Nations advocate, though the League was an organ of the Allies, which he had opposed during World War I.*

I

*F*rom here and there in Europe, and to some extent from America, I have in recent years heard from people who wanted me to write an aphorism for them, a word of wisdom according to which they could live in the future. And, each time, this thought occurred to me: Unfortunately, they have got the news that I am a wise man, so there is no point in my hiding it any longer—I have been found out!

I realize well enough that I am only one of many who have received that kind of request. Requests of that kind date from the time of world teach-ers such as Kant, Goethe, Darwin, and Tolstoy, and since great prophets are no longer living among us, people approach the small ones, of whom there are many, a dozen at least.

But that anybody should come to me! I who do not know how to rec-oncile myself with life, who have to ask directions from the sea, the wind, and the stars.

Others in our own time have been clever and have come out with one idea after another, Bergson with intuition, Einstein with the theory of relativity. I am blank, have no qualifications, know nothing, do not even have a diploma. I live as a peasant on his own soil, an "innocent abroad." An aphorism to live by, a word of wisdom? The ancients had Augustus's motto: Festina lente.

But these inquiries point clearly to one thing: the perplexing confusion that prevails among humanity. Everybody is groping about; nobody is at peace. God is forgotten, the almighty dollar seems to be taking His place, and machinery provides no relief to the soul. The way is closed. In the face of these conditions, America only increases its speed. America will not be stopped by any obstacle, but will move ahead, will force its way. Will America turn around? By no means. It will only speed up, move like a hurricane, drive its life up to a white-hot glow. We in Europe have the word *Americanism;* the ancients had *festina lente.*

It is not a sign of power to misuse it. In some cases it is not even a sign of power to use it. Power wears out, and there comes a day when it is exhausted and the reserve must be consumed. Ancient peoples such as the Assyrians and the Babylonians used their power, misused it, and fell to ruin.

The Orientals, it seems to me, stand high in ethical wisdom. From an early period they have been the fortunate possessors of contentment with life. Smiling at the restless squirming of the Occidentals, they bow their heads in contemplative quiet, satisfied with what they have.

Newspapers recently ran a story about an airplane that was forced to land in the desert. Natives of the oasis Sisdiokba, who had seen the great bird come down from the sky, gathered around the bird, thought for a while and shook their heads, but said nothing. The bird was dead; it had never been alive. The fliers had expected a different reception: utter amazement and a falling on the knees before the machine. No such thing happened. The fliers tried to interest the natives, telling them how many hours they had been in the air and how many were left to fly. Now they were going to restore the bird and resume their flight. The Berbers made some courteous remarks, said their farewells, and were ready to leave. This disappointed the fliers, who wanted to see kneeling and hear an outburst, who wished to tame these sons of the desert. Then the sheik expressed his doubt whether the invention, the trip, the whole idea was worth the amount of *human soul* that was used up by the undertaking.

Of course, his words had no effect on the fliers: his was a voice crying in the wilderness. But, two generations earlier, John Stuart Mill had written that there was a question whether the great mechanical inventions had lightened the burdens of life for a single human being. What would John Stuart Mill have said now!

Is sensation necessary for earthly life? The Berbers can live without it. We set records in flying, race driving, and fisticuffs. We howl to heaven with rapture over the heroes who fly across the Atlantic Ocean—and we go back home empty from our excitement. As long ago as 1860 the French tightrope walker Blondell [actually, Charles Blondin] walked on stilts on a rope stretched across Niagara Falls.

In such enterprises the qualities of personal energy, effort, ambition, and sensation stand out, but we show no spiritual balance when we applaud such a misunderstanding of what constitutes a truly heroic deed. We show civilization perhaps, but not culture. This is the fact: We become civilized, overcivilized, but we lose in spirit. During boxing matches we shamelessly expose ourselves with an insane, panicky rejoicing over the fighter who can do the most damage to his opponent.

When the daring—the foolhardy—aviator Lindbergh returned home from his Atlantic flight, American newspapers declared that he ought to be elected U.S. president. The young man, who stems from an old and honorable people, has himself reacted against and rejected foolish offers. He is popular, his name on everyone's lips, and he knows his machine, but president of the world's greatest and most powerful people? When such ideas can arise and be launched without embarrassment—is that culture?

An American author, a resident of New York, recently published an article in the great Danish newspaper *Politics* about a royal visit to the old Norwegian city of Trondhjem. He railed against its citizens for being so preoccupied with a visit from a king, and in a way he was perhaps justified. In the United States, however, I have observed a much greater excitement at a presidential visit to a town much smaller than Trondhjem and without its thousand-year history. But this is irrelevant, not worth wasting time on. The author also ridiculed as unimpressive the royal dwelling in Trondhjem and the rest of the buildings in the city—a subject he was not qualified to discuss. There stands in Trondhjem a wonderful Gothic cathedral, the grandest in Scandinavia, a noble structure that America cannot match and really never will. And the royal dwelling? It is no skyscraper, but it is a huge, elegantly furnished palace, the largest wooden building in the Scandinavian countries. Worth noting is the fact that it is constructed with varieties of wood that are as durable as masonry.

Surely the American author is what is called an educated man, one who has gone to his country's excellent schools and acquired up-to-date and accurate knowledge in diverse fields. It does not seem to occur to him, a civilized person, that he lacks anything in his education. But he lacks sympathy, a sense of history, patina. He did not go inside the royal dwelling, he relates, but he would not have been interested in its furnishings, anyhow, since these are not chintzy but have a certain nobility. In fact, a deep culture inheres in the wooden architecture of old Trondhjem.

II

Have I, myself, railed against America, run it down? I have not done that nor have I had reason to do so. To my dying day I will treasure what I learned during my two stays there, and I will always cherish the fine memories of those times. I am referring to American life and the nation as a whole.

I would like to mention the Americans' great helpfulness, their sympathy, their generosity. It is impossible to do justice here to a Rockefeller, a Carnegie, a Morgan, whose philanthropies are so vast that I have no means of evaluating them. I am thinking, rather, of the ordinary Americans' helpfulness in day-to-day life. They come immediately when needed, and they expect no reward for their good deeds. I once collected money to buy books for a small Norwegian community near the town where I was working. Dr. Booth [of English ancestry] was the first to sign up, and after him many others signed their names to the list, so many that I finally had to stop collecting.

I once worked for a relatively poor Irish farmer whose house caught fire. Neighbors came running from far and near; they not only helped to put out the fire but also rebuilt the house! We farm people could calmly go on with our work in the fields and, when the house was ready, thank the neighbors for their assistance and move in.

In this connection I may be allowed to relate a personal experience. During my travels when quite young I found myself in Chicago without money enough to get away from the city. So I wrote a brief note to a well-known American and asked for—*asked* for—twenty-five dollars that I could not promise to pay back. I took the letter and went all the way to the slaughter-houses, where I asked directions and found the man's office. It was an enormous room, barnlike and unattractive, but full of a monstrous swarm of office workers. At the entrance stood a young man as a doorkeeper, who took my letter and went off with it. I watched him make his way to the middle of the room, where a man sat on a raised platform working with papers. That was *Armour* [Philip Armour, the meatpacking baron]. No longer could I look up, doubtless feeling somewhat ashamed and also fearful of my probable rejection. Quickly the doorkeeper came back, so quickly I was not aware of him until he stood there and handed me twenty-five dollars. Slowly coming to my senses, I asked, idiotically: "I got them?" "Yes," said the man, smiling. "What did he say?" I asked. "He said your letter was worth it." I stood there fingering my bills for a while, then inquired: "Can I go up and thank him?" The man answered doubtfully: "Maybe. But that would probably just waste his time." I looked up at Mr. Armour, who did not even give me a glance but went on working with his papers.

I have no recollection of what I wrote in that letter, but it was surely the most wretched English that Mr. Armour had ever read, and he was certainly being ironic when he said it was worth twenty-five dollars.

Once, when I was working on the big Dalrymple farm in the Red River Valley, I had the following experience: A group of us workers was sent over to a new section. On the way a man became ill and had to be left in a small prairie town that we went through. When we had finished with the new section in the fall and came back to the prairie town, the sick man had recovered but was still weak and, having had no employment, was penniless and desperate. While I stood talking with him, a five-dollar bill was stuck in my hand, then another, and later several more—all to help out our unfortunate comrade.

I witnessed many, many other instances of American kindheartedness that I could add to those I have mentioned. True, a rich American can well afford it, but it nevertheless shows that he has a heart. And since the generosity, the helpfulness, is also universal among the ordinary, impecunious Americans, it is certainly nothing less than a national characteristic.

So we Europeans are shocked by the blind, uncomprehending hard-heartedness that certain American government policies imply. I am thinking of the terrible tariff walls erected against Europe and the ironfisted efforts to secure payment of Europe's war debt. As a layman, as a man in the street, I reason like this: Though America, for the moment, gains the most from its financial policy, what about the future, all the years to come, all the generations to be born? No more than any other country on the planet can America stand alone. America is not the world. America is a part of the world and must live its life together with all the other parts.

III

If I had more space at my disposal in this newspaper, I would hazard a few lines about the modern cultural life of America. There is an enormous difference between America's cultural life as it is today and as it was during my stay in the States in the 'eighties. It has always been tremendous, even gigantic in consequence of the nation's economic resources and intellectual power, but only in recent times has it reached a height worthy of this great people—now the recognized leaders in several branches of knowledge. On this subject I have no basis for an opinion except for the little I have learned through reading, and I offer no more than a general European view. The arts have risen to great heights, the pictorial art being rich and full of talent, and literature flowering, in particular the recent novelistic literature, which in the States is the freshest and most original in the world, a renaissance and a model for Europe. Schopenhauer has not been without influence there, nor has Nietzsche, but there are great independent cultural workers in American literature besides the writers of fiction, to mention only the pioneer of pragmatism William James.

If I had more room! I would have written about the delightful children and about the American women, the most beautiful feminine type on this earth. In my younger days I saw a bit of the world, setting foot in the land of the whites and in that of the coloreds, but never have I come across such perfect womanly beauties as in the big eastern cities of America. In facial features, in bodily form, in all limbs, in conduct, refinement, coquetry—in all respects a display of beauty, as I remember. And yet, as a common laborer, I never got a glimpse of the world of the upper class.

I will use the space I have left to pay my sincere tribute to the United States for what they have taught the world about the honor and glory of *work*. America works. America is teaching the world to be industrious. I am not thinking here of the forced effort to get ahead, with revolver in hand if necessary, nor am I thinking of the feverish working of the gold market or the shouting speculation on the stock market. I have in mind the ordinary American who has hands and a head to work with and uses both of them throughout his life. *But he uses them too hard.*

No one in America is too fine to do something, but the nation as a whole seems to work at a feverish and greedy tempo. I have read in Henry Ford's autobiography that he moved the machines in his factory close together to keep people from wasting time by walking a step farther than absolutely necessary. Time is money and money is everything. So runs the logic of thinking exclusively in terms of economic interest. In my time on the prairie we worked up to sixteen hours a day to get the harvesting done. Under these conditions we could only work like blacks, like slaves, and so we worked in a rough and ugly way, having no opportunity to do *beautiful* work, which has ethical value for the intelligent worker. On cold mornings we warmed up our oilcans by setting fire to a bunch of six wheat straws. We were in such a hurry that we did not have time to gather a pile of straw for a bonfire.

Life is short—but let us take time to live it! By toiling too hard we wear ourselves out and become useless before our time. Festina lente.

It seems that you Americans cannot be content with little. You want to have the best and the most. You want more than enough. The Orientals stand in contrast to this with their contentment, their inborn ability to do without. In Persia I saw a coachman sitting on his driver's seat and munching alternately on a slice of bread and a cluster of grapes. That was their lunch; they could do without meat. They could also do without a gold-cased pocket watch. I asked my coachman when we would be in the next town. He looked at the sun and answered: "We should be there in the big heat" (the heat of midday), a poetic time of day, almost like a line of verse.

The Americans will reply that no comparison is possible here, that a Ford car would have covered that short distance in less than an hour. Persia is one thing, progress another. Yes indeed, my coachman drove a horse, which he had time for and which suited him, and he would pause along the way with his horse, like a good companion. He asked the horse whether it would not hurry up a little, whether it was not ashamed of itself. "Look at the sun," he said. "Would you rather burn up?"

Progress—what is it? Is it the ability to drive faster on the roads? No, no, that would leave a deficit in the balance sheet of human accounting. Progress is the needed rest for the body and serenity for the soul. Progress is the well-being of humanity.

My First Time Abroad

Hamsun wrote his last book, On Overgrown Paths *(1949), recounting his treatment after World War II, to demonstrate that he was still of sound mind and had not supported the Nazis because of mental illness. Toward the end of the book he digressed to reminisce about his earliest experiences in the United States. Compulsive storyteller that he was, he departed from strict recollection to tell the story of Bridget and Patrick, largely a work of conscious, creative authorship.*

A recollection from my first time abroad occurs to me. No, nothing important or remarkable—just a series of simple, day-to-day experiences in the alien surroundings of a dreary little prairie town [Elroy, Wisconsin]. There was no river there and no forest, only a bit of brushwood. Things went well enough while I worked on the farm of some decent, ordinary people, but I suffered from homesickness and cried a lot. Smiling indulgently, the farmwife taught me the word *homesick.*

When I had worked there a few months, my employers, the Lovelands, could not afford to keep me any longer. We separated reluctantly, and it was late in the day when I set out for town. I was in no hurry. There was no road, only a path, and from time to time I sat down, to daydream. It was not like home when water ran under the melting ice here, the little pulsations under the ice not nearly so blue or so beautiful. So I shed another tear or two.

I heard steps on the path. A young woman. I knew her; she was the daughter of a widow in the neighborhood. A couple of times the widow had asked me to work for her whenever I finished at the Lovelands.

"Hello, Noot. Did I scare you?"

"No."

"I'm going to town," she said.

She was carrying a churn paddle that had come loose from the shaft. I offered to carry the apparatus, which I was well acquainted with from my childhood at home, and which I could easily have fixed with my pocket-knife if I had had a little piece of dry wood.

She kept chatting and twittering all the time, and I kept trying to answer with the few English words I knew. This was so annoying that I wished she was dead and buried.

"Phew!" I said. "It must still be a long way to town."

"Yes, I hope so," the little witch replied, laughing. She had nothing against walking along and twittering.

We came to Larsen's workshop in the town. It was beginning to get dark.

"Dear Noot, now you must go back with me," said Bridget.

"What!" I exclaimed, gaping.

"It's getting too dark for me to go by myself," she said.

Larsen, a Dane, agreed that I must go with her.

So we started back. It grew darker and darker, until we finally had to go hand in hand, watching out for the twigs that kept striking us in the face. But it was a nice hand to hold onto.

"We forgot the churn paddle!" I suddenly cried out.

"That doesn't matter." Bridget answered.

"It doesn't matter?"

"No. I've got you with me."

Why did she say that? I could only take it to mean she liked me a lot and, indeed, was crazy about me.

When we arrived at her home I wanted to turn around immediately, but did not manage to do so. I must have something to eat—dinner—and must stay overnight, Bridget showing me a cubbyhole with a bed in it. In the morning the mother and daughter persuaded me to settle down and work for them for a while, and I looked around the farm a bit. There were two mules and three cows. "There's no help to be had," the widow complained. As for me, I was not used to working by myself. At the Lovelands there was the husband to lead me, but here were only womenfolk to point out the most important things to be done. Of course, I could not simply walk away, so I chopped up a big pile of firewood and later took to hauling out manure with the mules. This went on for days.

But the widow, realizing that she must look for better help, went to town one day and came back with a Finn, a capable fellow from Osterbotten who really knew his stuff. Young Bridget no longer seemed so happy at having got me, nor did she look at me and hold my hand any more.

Oh, I knew God's word from my distant homeland, but nevermore in this life would I put any trust in a woman's word.

There continued to be a serious labor shortage. When I went back to town a farmer stopped me on the street and wanted me to go with him. He could probably tell by my clothes and otherwise that I was a newcomer, and I was not wrong in thinking I was in great demand. I went along with the man, who was driving a wagon with two big horses. As soon as we got home he set me to work. I was to dig a little grave, only a few feet long, at the edge of the woods. This took no time at all, and when I had finished with it the man came out with a tiny coffin on his shoulder and set it down in the grave. That took no time, either, and as I waited for new instructions he motioned for me to fill up the grave and lay the sod on top of it. Then he left.

But, for God's sake, wasn't he coming back? No. He was working with something in the outbuildings, apparently quite busy.

I marveled and shuddered and felt sad. A child's body had been put in the ground—that was all. No ceremony, not even a stanza from a hymn. They were young people I was with, the farmer and his wife, but I could not talk with them about it, and I never found out what kind of church they belonged to.

Otherwise, I had nothing to complain about. Here were a well-kept house and yard, horses and cows, beautiful soil, no children. My job was easy. While the husband took care of the animals and did the milking, I did the cultivating, as did the wife, who was round and fat and quick to laugh. She taught me many English words and gave me a little room, with a window and a bed, to live in. Rare spirits, they tried to weigh me on a scale, but I broke the thing and brought the yardarm down on my head. It puzzled me the way they made a fuss over me and bragged about me because I was so heavy. When the wife went to town to sell butter and wheat and do some shopping, I was now and then assigned to go with her and drive.

When the spring planting was done, the man wanted to keep me longer, and I stayed until after the harvesting. That must have been about 1880 or 1881 [actually 1882]. As I got used to the couple, I began to feel more and more at home. Their name was Spear and they were both of German descent. We shook hands with a firm grip when I finally left.

Another man, a stranger, waylaid me and offered a whole winter's employment cutting railroad ties. I refused. The man then offered me his own little farm to rent. When I would not do that either, he wanted to sell me on credit a team of horses and a wagon for hauling freight. He was full of expedients and speculations, and I had a hard time getting rid of him.

One day I received the offer of a job as "delivery boy" for a business in the town. I accepted that offer. I carried packages and boxes to addresses around the town, and after completing a circuit I went back to the store. It was the biggest business in the place, with several men behind the counter. The owner, named Hart, was an Englishman. We sold everything imaginable, from green soap to silk cloth, canned goods, thimbles, and stationery. I could not help learning the names of all our wares, and my vocabulary made gratifying progress. After a while the boss hired a new man for my job as delivery boy and let me take a place behind the counter in the store. I now wore a suit and shiny shoes, had a rented room in town, and ate at one of the hotels. The farm people, those with whom I had become acquainted earlier, were amazed to see how high I had risen in the world.

When young Bridget the farm girl came into the store and saw my new respectability, she may have regretted, and continued to regret to her dying day, that she had ever broken off with me. Perhaps. I don't know. I did know that she wanted to talk to me outside. She said: "Dear Noot, will you be so kind as to help me with all my packages?" "With the greatest pleasure," I replied. I could easily have motioned to the new delivery boy to do this work, but instead, to my own wonderment, I said: "With the greatest pleasure"! So I personally carried her packages out and put them in the wagon. After brushing the dust off my clothes, I courteously asked about her mother and the farm and the Finn.

Oh, the Finn was gone and the harvesting over. But her mother was not going to struggle with farm work any longer. She intended to sell the farm, move to town, and go into the business of serving cookies, chocolate, and lemonade. Bridget was quite excited. They had already picked out a rickety building, a mere shack, that could be fixed up as their restaurant.

Here enters my friend Patrick. An Irishman, somewhat older than I, Pat was an adventurer, comrade, and rare fellow. Like me, he lived in a little attic room in town. We often talked together, both of us suffering from homesickness and determined to go back home just as soon as we could afford to.

Pat, who may have had a little experience with house construction in his homeland, did not object to being called an architect. He now figured out the size of the restaurant, being careful to get the number of feet and inches just right. He obtained lumber and, from my store, nails and cardboard. Then he went industriously ahead.

Pat and I had quite a bit in common and saw each other every day. Now and then one of us might have a dollar that the other needed, and we also lent books back and forth, but our reciprocal book lending did not amount to much. I did not know enough English to read Paine's *Age of Reason,* and he did not understand J. P. Jacobsen's *Marie Grubbe,* which I had bought in Chicago. Those were youthful, aspiring, hardworking days, but we never forgot that we would eventually get away from this land and go home. Privately we cried and felt sorry for ourselves.

Don't think Bridget threw herself on the ground and moaned when her childhood home was sold! A path led off from the farm to the forest, and the little birds in the trees were now left behind. There were flowers and heavenly rain in the spring and a breeze rustling through the fields of grain on a summer day. Had Bridget forgotten all that? There was also the lovely little creek that ran across the whole farm, and now it had been sold. Good God, to sell the creek! The farmhouse brooded, realizing what had happened, as the unpainted plank wall looked back at her. She ought to have laid her cheek against that wall and never have gone off and left it.

"We'll never understand these people over here," Pat said. "They do things that would make us sad if we did them. Last year I worked on a farm in Wyoming. The man kept studying the printed circulars and pictures that he got in the mail. One day he said to me: 'I'm leaving right away!' Then he took his family and moved to Florida. Gave up his farm in Wyoming and moved to Florida."

"No, Pat, we don't understand these people. We'll get away from here."

"But Bridget is a sweet girl," said Pat.

"What do you mean by that?" I asked.

"She's a sweet girl. I'm now working for her and her mother. They're going to start a restaurant. You don't really know Bridget."

"So that's how it is!" I said.

But from that day on I had my doubts about Pat and his longing to go back to his homeland. We talked about it. Pat said that, yes indeed, he was still eager to go home to Erin, and he tallied up its glories and its greatness. There were miles and miles of green grass with more sheep and cattle and churches and castles than anyone could count.

I listened and nodded and said we had the same things in Norway.

But Pat, tasting blood, declared that no other country could compare with Erin, which had mountain chains that ran through twenty counties and almost out into the Atlantic Ocean. And it had great rivers and cities and inland seas with ships on them—and processions headed by cardinals.

Nodding in agreement with much of this, I repeated that we had it, too. Pat and I went on bragging about our respective homelands. I mentioned Galdhøpiggen, the highest mountain in Norway. Lomseggen. "There stands a church in Lomseggen," I said, "and in that church I was confirmed in 1873."

This, which would have stirred the emotions of a stone, had no effect on Pat. He had tasted more blood, and he now talked like a wild man. He claimed that an Irishman had invented a machine for flying in the air. Yes, sir. And he further stretched the truth about a basalt mine in Antrim—he was himself from Antrim, he said, and the hole went all the way down to the center of the earth. His patriotism knew no bounds. He expatiated on the olive groves and rose gardens and the fly-fishermen who sat shoulder to shoulder along all the rivers—

"Ha-ha, fly-fishermen!" I interrupted. Had he never heard about our fishermen, about Lofoten and Finnmark?

No.

And all the other things we have, besides. Were our great forests and waterfalls of no account? "Hold your tongue, Pat." Wasn't it true that we had discovered America four hundred years before Columbus? And wasn't it true that our country's present borders extend all the way to Russia?

"To Russia?" exclaimed Pat, who did not believe me.

Okay. The main thing was that both of us longed to be back in our homelands. But I still had doubts about Pat.

Doubts about Pat? Didn't he keep on working like a dog and living in an attic room with only a little kerosene lamp for light? His folks ought to know about that, his father and mother ought to know about it. But he had not wanted to write home and tell them. He who had two riding horses in the stall at home—and here had a sloping ceiling with a small iron-framed window to lift up.

"Do you really have riding horses at home?"

"That surprises you. Do you know how many windows there are in our main building? Many more than in this whole town. And when I stick my head through the roof here, I see nothing but clotheslines on the back of a lot. You have no idea how these clotheslines bother me, the way they run zigzag with waving and fluttering clothes, while I have to sit and try to draw straight lines in planning my architectural work. But I keep at it for Bridget's sake, because Bridget is a sweet girl."

"How can you go home when you tie yourself to a girl here?"

"I'll take her with me," said Pat.

"You'll take her with you?"

"Sure. Do you think I would go off and leave her? If you do, you don't know me. I'll simply take her along."

"I want to see that," I said.

But now things began to go completely awry. They could hardly have gone worse.

The clotheslines belonged to Kleist, the baker, whose bakery was on the front of the lot. One night Pat went out and untied all the lines and laid them neatly on the ground. The next morning there was quite a row. Kleist, an Austrian from Vienna, was a nice, mild, middle-aged man, but he was not going to put up with this kind of shenanigans. He had a serious talk with Pat, who explained that he was not playing a trick but was getting rid of a nuisance. "Can't you stand to look at clotheslines?" Kleist asked. "No," said Pat. "Ha-ha," laughed the Austrian, taking it as a joke. And he tied the clotheslines back up.

But it turned out to be more than a joke.

It just happened that young Bridget, the girl from the farm, became the baker's student, learning how to bake all kinds of cakes and rolls and Vienna bread and such things for her restaurant. This was perhaps a smart idea of the mother and daughter, one that would pay for itself, and it went quite well for a while. Pat never had anything to say about it.

But gradually it began to go wrong.

The restaurant, once it opened, enjoyed great success. Pat the architect had turned the shack into a suitable building, which, to be sure, had only one main room, with places to sit and drink lemonade and chocolate, but also had an addition for the kitchen and bakery. Overhead were a few small private rooms in which the mother and daughter lived.

The baker, too, deserved something for the assistance he had given them, but he went too far. He could not control himself and act his age; he began to feel too young. His children having grown up and left home, he probably took, at first, a fatherly interest in the pretty young woman who wanted to learn his trade and was so clever at it. Anyhow, he helped to install a huge stove with baking ovens and sheets, thus converting the addition into a bakery.

Well and good. But the old fellow began to wash clothes for Bridget. He always had hot as well as cold water in his huge kettles, and when he washed the dough off his own baking clothes he could throw in Bridget's. Realizing that she did not have much money, he wanted to help her. His intentions may have been good, but he went too far and thus aroused the anger of Pat. What Kleist the baker did was to include little aprons and dickeys and handkerchiefs that could not possibly be his own. And he hung them on those clotheslines on his lot!

Pat came to me at the store and wanted me to go with him. He was pale as a ghost.

"You should get another room and move out," I told him.

"You can't mean that," Pat replied. "I need a place where I can keep a lookout."

We went to the baker. Pat wanted to buy the lot but could not afford it, and Kleist would not sell it anyhow.

"What's wrong with you?" Kleist asked. "I must wash clothes and hang them up to dry. I have to be clean and snow white all day. Can't you understand that?"

"What about all those women's things that you hang there?" said Pat. "You swine!"

"Can't you stand to look at women's things?" Kleist asked.

"No," said Pat.

The Austrian roared with laughter.

Though Pat badly wanted revenge, he could only stand there with his lips quivering. After a while he solemnly threatened his enemy with severe action. He would let his relatives in Erin know what had happened, he said, and they belonged to the nobility.

This did not make much of an impression on Kleist, who looked mystified, then nodded and left.

"You have to move," I told Pat. "You can see that this won't work."

"I'm not moving," Pat insisted.

No, of course not. He had not yet acted idiotic enough, crazy enough. I was annoyed with him and let him know it. I could not understand this new side of Pat. I saw how desperately and comically in love he was—but what did nobility have to do with it? That might have been something fine in Ireland, but just what it was I did not know. I made fun of him, telling him he was so preoccupied with his little farmer's daughter that he had taken leave of his senses.

"I'd be willing to die for her," he said.

That was magnificent. "And you are of the nobility," I casually remarked.

"It's not me that's of the nobility," he said, "it's my mother."

He took a letter out of his pocket and showed it to me. On the back of the envelope was a little figure in green enamel that he called a noble coat of arms. It looked very nice, anyhow. Not knowing anything about it, I said nothing in response, but it puzzled me. Changing the subject, I began to kid him about his two riding horses.

"Dear Noot," he answered, "you don't understand these things at all. We have an estate, so I could have riding horses."

This did not enable me to understand things any better.

From now on Pat would stick his head out the skylight all day, keeping an eye on the clothes hanging out to dry. He went crazy, driven by a jealousy so overwhelming that he could not get over it. I laughed at him, but this had no effect. His eyes took on an extremely crafty look. No one was going to fool him; more women's things might come, but not a single piece would escape his notice.

The perfect fool.

For quite a while Kleist the baker gave instructions in his art of baking, but one day he declared that young Bridget was fully trained and quite capable of making cookies on her own at home in the restaurant. Then came a denouement.

By no means a bad person, but a kindly old Viennese and a master of his craft, Kleist was proud of his apt pupil. He refused to accept any pay for his instruction, living well enough, as he did, from the excellent business he did with the townspeople. And now, after some months, he resumed his ordinary day-to-day life. Nothing had happened between him and Bridget.

Pat now underwent a tremendous change: he was no longer in love with Bridget. It was a miracle. Ah, what a miracle! He was no longer in love with Bridget!

He who had been so deeply enamored, so terribly smitten, who had recently talked of dying for her—how was this change to be explained? The explanation was quite simple: he had nothing and nobody to be jealous of any more, nothing to provoke him any longer, so his ardor was dampened and his violent feelings exhausted.

Poor Pat. He had become thin and emaciated, because he had not had time to eat while keeping watch at his skylight. But now he quickly got a grip on himself and straightened up. He did indeed.

We went together to the restaurant. Pat did not say anything as we drank our chocolate and ate our cookies. No longer restrained by love, Pat suggested when we paid that he now needed his own pay. Mother and daughter looked up in amazement. This was a side of Pat they had not seen before. What a difference!

Pay—really? Well, yes, for the work he had done. But couldn't he come and live up above, in one of the small rooms he had built?

Pat shook his head.

Then why had he made those small rooms?

Pat said: "I need my money. I'm going to take a trip to Wyoming."

They were not only unwilling but quite irritated, Bridget especially. Having been pampered by her fatherly friend Kleist, she now had fancy ideas.

I was annoyed at her; she had gotten too smart. Nowadays she pranced around in city clothes, but she had shown no regret when her childhood home was sold. No, she was not nice.

I said to her: "I went by Larsen's workshop the other day. Your churn paddle is still there."

"So what?"

"It's your churn paddle. You've never picked it up."

"No, I never have—my churn paddle—I have no use for it—you can have it, Noot. Ha-ha!"

"I got nothing in return for carrying it for you," I said.

"Hush, Bridget," said her mother.

"It comes to $240 for my labor," said Pat.

Mother and daughter consulted one another. "We'll get an appraisal for the work," they said, treating Pat shamefully. Oh, they knew what they were doing. The appraisal took time, while Pat needed the money right away. Finally he had to settle for half of what was due him, just to get what he could. "Cheapskates!" said Pat.

Anyhow, I was much relieved that he had broken off with Bridget, and we again sat and discussed our future. Now that spring was coming, we were anxious to go home. For my part, I wanted to quit my job at the store, where I had been for three years with a small salary that would never amount to much. I wanted to go out west to the prairie, where I would get board and would have no expenses while working.

"That won't amount to anything, either," said Pat. "I'm going to Wyoming."

"What will you do there?"

"Look around a bit. I can sell the farm, you know."

"What farm?"

"The one I worked on."

"Was it your farm?"

"Yeah, the man left it and went to Florida."

Speechless, I looked at him and thought: Did that make it your farm? Pat, Pat, you are a strange character, one of the strangest adventurers under the sun. Now I'm confused about you again.

"I'll sell it anyhow," he said.

"Well, you probably have a right to," I said. "You have back wages due you for your work on the farm."

"Yeah," said Pat, grabbing at the idea.

"I can understand that. You've worked long and hard and never got anything for it."

"Yeah," said Pat.

I nodded and said that was plain to see. "You were there a long time, too, maybe for ages."

"A year and a half," said Pat.

"Of course. So there's nothing wrong with it. I'm glad you told me. Remember to give me your address before you leave."

Once Pat had left, the town seemed a more disagreeable place than ever. He was an indispensable companion, and I missed him. I wrote to him a couple of times, but got no answer. Maybe he didn't have time, or maybe he was busy thinking of his trip home. Finally, at the end of my days in the town, Mr. Hart offered me a decent raise if I would stay. It was too late.

I went to Dalrymple's farm in the Red River Valley and was there until the harvest was over.

Bibliographical Notes

Introduction: Hamsun's America

This account is derived largely from Harald S. Næss, *Knut Hamsun og Amerika* (Knut Hamsun and America) (Oslo: Gyldendal, 1969), and Robert Ferguson, *Enigma: The Life of Knut Hamsun* (New York: Farrar, Straus & Giroux, 1987). Ferguson lists Næss in his bibliography but does not cite him in his notes and appears not to have used his book. He omits some facts that Næss includes but supplies quite a bit of information that Næss does not. The two works, which generally agree, supplement one another very well. Both Næss and Ferguson, however, are perhaps too prone to accept Hamsun's imaginative reminiscences as reliable sources for his life in the United States.

An earlier biography, Einar Skavlan, *Knut Hamsun* (Oslo: Gyldendal, 1929), is also helpful. After quoting a friend of Hamsun on the latter's losing track of street names when a streetcar conductor in Chicago, Skavlan comments: "One can hear Hamsun's own joking, boasting, ironical voice in this description of his incompetence" (115). But the biography by Hamsun's son Tore is of little use for the subject's American experience. Tore begins his account of this experience with Hamsun's arrival in Madison, Wisconsin, "en sommerdag" (it was actually in February) and proceeds to make other dubious or erroneous statements.

Tore Hamsun undoubtedly was misled by the *Life Story of Rasmus B. Anderson,* written by Anderson with the assistance of Albert O. Barton, pages 304–19 of which deal with Hamsun (the book was published by the author in Madison, Wis., c. 1915; I cite the second edition of 1917). With regard to Hamsun's first appearance in Madison, Anderson writes, "One day in the summer of 1882, I think . . ." (305). Displaying a weak memory but a strong sense of self-importance, Anderson makes other obvious errors. To mention only a few examples, he says it was he who advised his young visitor to use the name Hamsund instead of Pedersen: "This advice he at once accepted" (307). He implies that he got Hamsun a job in Elroy and thus was responsible for his going there, and he baldly avers that he recommended Hamsun to Kristofer Janson and thus was responsible for his getting the job in Minneapolis (305–6).

Writers on Hamsun generally mention his debt to Mark Twain. Trygve Braatøy, *Livets cirkel: Bidrag til analyse av Knut Hamsuns diktning* (The circle of life: A contribution to the analysis of Knut Hamsun's writing) (Oslo: Cappelens, 1954), states: "Mark Twain is the only teacher that everyone agrees Hamsun has had" (98). This seems to overlook Bjørnstjerne Bjørnson, who served as the earliest model for the young Hamsun.

Steven H. Rossel, *A History of Scandinavian Literature, 1870–1980*, trans. Anne C. Ulmer (Minneapolis: University of Minnesota Press, 1982), provides the following explanation for Hamsun's Nazism: "Hamsun's mystical attachment to the soil, his glorification of the superman, inspired by Nietzsche, his anti-Americanism, and his success in Germany . . . all of these elements drove him into the arms of national socialism" (103). These elements are relevant, but omitted here is the most important of all—his Anglophobia.

The quotation exemplifying this Anglophobia is from *Den siste Glæde* (The last joy) (Christiania and Copenhagen: Gyldendalske Boghandel, 1912), and reads as follows in the original: "Mig vørde de ikke de to Englænder I Gjeitfjøset, jeg var bare en av de Indfødte, en Nordmand, jeg hadde at tie til de mægtige Turister. Men selv tilhørte de den Nation av Løpere, Vognstyrere og Last som den sunde Skjæbne fra Tyskland en Dag vil tukte til Døden" (70). The English translation of this book is titled *Look Back on Happiness* (New York, 1940), according to Arvid Østby, *Knut Hamsun—en bibliografi* (Oslo: Gyldendal, 1972), 30.

Fra det moderns Amerikas Aandsliv (On the cultural life of modern America) (Copenhagen: P. G. Philipsens Forlag, 1889) made little impression in the United States except among Norwegian Americans, as it was eighty years before an English translation of the book appeared. This was edited and translated by Barbara Gordon Morgridge and was published by the Harvard University Press in 1969. I have not seen the Morgridge translation and have translated all the quotations independently; these are from pages 6–11 and 18–19 of the original.

The book that Hamsun mistakenly attributed to Zachary Taylor is Bayard Taylor, *Northern Travel: Summer and Winter Pictures of Sweden, Denmark and Lapland* (New York: G. P. Putnam, 1860). Taylor accuses the Norwegians of the same fault for which Hamsun blames the Americans: "Perhaps the most general feature of the Norwegian character is an excessive national vanity. Say everything you like, except that Norway in any respect is surpassed by any other country" (327).

The conversation between Edevart and August is from *August* (2 vols., Oslo: Gyldendal, 1930), 2:234:

Efter en Stund sa Edevart: Det blir vel til det at du kommer til Amerika igjen?

Ja det gjør du ikke tvile paa! svarte August. Det er ikke nogen anden Verdensdel for en Mand som mig.

The discussion of August's traits is found in 2:243–47 of the same novel.

For an enlightening discussion of the conservative anticapitalistic movement on the part of intellectuals, see Peter Nicolaisen, "The Southern Agrarians and European Agrarianism," *Mississippi Quarterly* 49 (Fall 1996): 683–700.

Critical Reporting (1885–1888)

These newspaper articles were collected and reissued in Knut Hamsun, *Over haveet: artikler og rejsebreve* (Across the sea: Articles and travel letters), ed. Lars Frode Larsen (Copenhagen: Brøndum, 1990). A Norwegian version was published by Gyldendal in Oslo in 1990; my translation is based on the Danish edition.

The first two articles were originally titled simply "Fra Amerika" (From America); the third was "Fra en Indianerleir" (From an Indian camp); and the fifth "Et Gårdsbrug I det Fjerne Vest" (A farm in the far West).

The first eight paragraphs of the essay on the Indian camp, in which Hamsun comments on Indians in general, have been omitted from the translation. The notes are Hamsun's, as they appeared in the original publication.

Memory and Fantasy (1897–1905)

"Rædsel" (Fear, or terror), "Paa Prærien" (On the prairie), and "Zachæus" were included in Hamsun's collection *Kratskog: Historier og Skitser* (Brushwood: Stories and sketches) (Copenhagen: Gyldendalske Boghandels Forlag, 1903), 53–78, 81–90, 117–31. My translation is based on that source.

In 1924, some forty years after his frightening experience in Madelia, Hamsun wrote to Henry Johnston: "Do you remember that I, one night in Madelia, was broken into? I do not blame you if you doubt whether this really happened. I had my own suspicion as to the person who did it—or had it done—and this suspicion has not weakened through time." Næss suggests that Hamsun suspected a competitor of Johnston's in the local lumber business (*Knut Hamsun and America*, 42).

A small part of "Paa Prærien" was published in an English translation, under the title "The Prairie," in *Living Age* 310 (August 27, 1921): 349–50. That selection ends with Hamsun and his fellow farmhands heading for town, "where we could get a train to take us still farther west"—a mistranslation of *Østen*. The clause should read: "a train that would take us back East again."

"Vagabonds Dage" (Vagabond days) and "Kvindesejr" (A woman's victory) were included in Hamsun's collection *Stridende Liv: Skildringer fra Vesten og Østen* (Striving life: Depictions from the West and the East) (Copenhagen and Christiania: Gyldendalske, 1905), 99–112, 115–187, and my translation is based on that source.

According to Ferguson, the story of the woman's victory "contains a number of interesting details of Hamsun's life as a conductor." In particular, "he was in that hard winter unable to afford warm clothing, and . . . adopted the tramp's habit of wearing a layer of newspapers next to his skin. His fellow workers . . . enjoyed making him crackle by poking him with their fingers" (*Enigma*, 83). But the photograph taken of him in his conductor's uniform—consisting of a vest, a woolen jacket, and a heavy overcoat—shows him to have been warmly clad (see frontispiece). The crackling newspaper was part of his fantasy, not part of his actual experience on the streetcars.

Hamsun seems to have remembered the experience with a certain fondness and pride. In *I Æventyrland* (In wonderland) (Copenhagen: Gyldendalske, 1903), he tells of a train ride in the Caucasus Mountains: "Vi gaar med et ganske sagte og jeg kunde med Øvelse fra min Konductortid I Amerika hoppe af Toget og gribe den sidste Vogn og hoppe paa igen" (All at once we were going quite slowly and, with my practice as a conductor in America, I could jump off the train, grab the last car, and jump back on) (52).

The five stories in this section are discussed and four of them are translated in Sverre Arestad, "Hamsun and America," *Norwegian-American Studies* 24 (1970): 148–92. My translations are completely independent of Arestad's, which came to my attention only after I had finished my work.

Mellow Reminiscence (1928, 1949)

The essay "Festina Lente" was reprinted in Hamsun, *Artikler* (Articles), ed. Francis Bull (Oslo: Gyldendal, 1939), 217–29, and my translation is based on this source. The essay also appeared in a later edition of the same collection under the title *Artikler 1889–1928* (Oslo: Gyldendal, 1966), 141–48.

"My First Time Abroad" is from Hamsun's *Paa gengrodde Stier* (On overgrown paths) (Oslo: Gyldendal, 1949), 165–82. An English translation of this book by Carl L. Anderson (New York: Paul S. Eriksson, 1967) is listed by Ostby (*Hamsun bibliografi*, 39). I have not seen the Anderson translation. In the book, the story of Bridget and Patrick has no heading; I have supplied the present title.

Though to some extent based on Hamsun's actual experiences, the story departs from the facts in several respects. For example, it concludes with Hamsun's immediate departure for Dakota, which did not occur until several years later. It describes Elroy as a "dreary little prairie town," but Elroy is located in Wisconsin's scenic Driftless Area, where, except for the absence of a coast, the topography is not very different from that of southern Norway around Nørholm, Hamsun's residence from 1918 until his death. While giving top roles to more or less imaginary characters, Hamsun neglects to mention a number of people who figured prominently in his life in Wisconsin.